Die Militair-Musik
und die militair-musikalische
Organisation
eines Kriegsheeres

The Military Band and the musical organization of an army

The Military Band and the musical organization of an army

The bequeathed memoir of

Wilhelm Wieprecht

former director of all the music of the
Royal Prussian Guard Corps.

Together with the appendix:

Wieprecht's report on the victory of the music
of the Prussian Guards in the international
competition of European military music
at the Paris World's Fair in 1867.

Translated by Craig Dabelstein

Maxime's Music

Originally published in German as *Die Militair-Musik und die militair-musikalische Organisation eines Kriegsheeres* by Carl Habel, 1885.
This edition copyright © 2024 by Craig Dabelstein.
ISBN: 978-1-936512-95-9
Published by Maxime's Music.

MAXIMESMUSIC.COM

Contents

I Deutsch	1
Vorwort	3
Erster Theil	5
Zweiter Theil	17
Anhang	27
II English	35
Preface	37
Chapter 1	39
Chapter 2	51
Appendix	61

Part I

Deutsch

Vorwort

Die nachfolgende Denkschrift stammt aus der Hinterlassenschaft des bekannten ehemaligen Directors der gesammten Musik des preußischen Garde-Corps, W. Wieprecht, gest. 4. August 1872 zu Berlin. Es war seine letzte Arbeit. Er übergab dieselbe nicht lange vor seinem Tode dem Schriftsteller Herrn Friedrich Bücker, welcher einige Jahre vorher die Biographie Wieprechts für das „Daheim" geschrieben hatte, mit der Bitte um dereinstige Veröffentlichung, wenn dieser einen geeigneten Zeitpunkt dafür als passend erachte, und zwar ohne jede Einschränkung. Als Veranlassung der Denkschrift erzählte er Herrn Bücker, daß dieselbe die Lösung eines Versprechens sei, welches er dem Kaiser Napoleon III. von Frankreich nach dem Siege der Musik der preußischen Garde in Paris gegeben, als der Kaiser ihm den Orden der Ehrenlegion überreichte und ihn zur Tafel gezogen. Er versprach dem Kaiser, über die Zwecke und Organisation einer Heeresmusik eine ausführliche Denkschrift zu verfassen, löste auch das Versprechen und beabsichtigte, das Schriftstück in Paris persönlich zu überreichen. Mehrfache Krankheit aber und dienstliche Angelegenheiten verhinderten die Reise, und endlich machte der deutsch-französische Krieg die Ausführung des Planes überhaupt unmöglich.

In gleicher Weise findet sich diese Denkschrift auch in einem Briefe Wieprecht's an Herrn Professor Ferdinand Sieber erwähnt.

Herr Bücker glaubt nun mit der Veröffentlichung nicht länger zögern zu sollen, und die Verlagshandlung kommt seinem Anerbieten gern nach, da die Gedanken des berühmten Reorganisators der preußischen Militairmusik, über eine Centralisation derselben u.s.w. bei allen Heeren und Militairmusikfreunden das größte Interesse erregen werden und die eingehendste Beachtung verdienen.

Erster Theil

Das Instrumentalwesen der Militairmusik

§ 1.

Eine gut organisirte Militairmusik bildet nicht nur einen integrirenden Theil des gesammten Armee-Wesens jeder Nation, sondern sie darf auch als dasjenige Moment eines Heeres betrachtet werden, welches, wie kaum ein anderes, das Soldaten herz hebt und stärkt. Sie ist der treueste Begleiter des Kriegers, fie führt mit tactgemäßem Tonspiel seine Märsche an, fie begeistert ihn mit feurigen Klängen zum todverachtenden Sturm auf den Feind, fie ersetzt ihm die Orgel zum Gesange beim Feld-Gottesdienst, sie geleitet den geschiedenen Helden mit klagendem Trauermarsch zur letzten Ruhestätte und feiert in jauchzenden Tonweisen den errungenen Sieg.

Soll die Militairmusik aber ihren militairischen und musikalischen Aufgaben gleichmäßig genügen, so muß sie sowohl in Bezug auf Besetzung der Stimmen, als auch auf deren Schulung und Leitung — vor Allem aber auf die Anwendung geeigneter Instrumente gut organisirt sein. Wie dies zu bewerkstelligen, das soll die nachfolgende Denkschrift darzulegen versuchen, welche aus den Erfahrungen einer vierzig jährigen treuen und kunstbegeisterten Wirksamkeit auf diesem Felde hervorgegangen ist.

§ 2.

Wir wollen uns zunächst mit den der Militairmusik unentbehrlichen und allein für sie geeigneten Instrumenten beschäftigen, und im zweiten Theile dieser Abhandlung alsdann die Art und Weise der militairischen und musikalischen Organisation der Musikmannschaften in's Auge fassen.

In den drei ursprünglichen und der Militairmusik von den ersten Anfängen an eigenen Instrumenten: der Trommel, der Querpfeife und dem Signalhorn sind auch die drei Hauptfactoren der Militairmusik: der Rhythmus, die Melodie und die Harmonie vertreten.

§ 3.

Aus der Masse der **Schlagwerkzeuge**, die schon in den ältesten Zeiten den Zweck hatten, das rhythmische Element darzustellen, hat sich unsere moderne Wirbeltrommel als ein, den Kriegsheeren ganz unentbehrliches Instrument erwiesen. Sie regelt da, wo Melodie und Harmonie fehlen, durch mannigfach rhythmische Klangfiguren den Schritt des Soldaten, ruft die durch angestrengte Märsche ermüdeten Krieger zu erneuter Lebensfrische auf und begeistert die Colonnen zum Sturm auf den Feind.

Aus der einfachen Trommel ging eine ganze Reihe anderer Schlagwerkzeuge hervor, von denen wir hier nur die Handtrommel (Tambourin), die große Trommel (Militairpauke) und die Kesselpauken (Timpani) anführen, welche sämmtlich, mit Ausnahme des Tambourin, Aufnahme in die Militairmusik gefunden haben. Es dürfte hier am Platze sein, auch des Triangels, der Becken und des Glockenspieles zu gedenken, einer Gattung von Schlagwerkzeugen, die — wie ja auch die Militairpauke, welche wir natürlich neben der Wirbeltrommel nennen mußten — von den Orientalen auf uns gekommen sind, wovon der Name „Janitscharenmusik" noch heute Zeugniß giebt.

§ 4.

Es konnte aber nicht fehlen, daß der Krieger neben dem rhythmischen Elemente sehr bald ein Verlangen nach Melodie empfand. Deshalb mag er sich anfänglich auf dem Marsche seine heimathlichen Lieder gepfiffen oder auch gesungen haben; später ward diesem Drange nach Melodie neben dem Schall der Trommel vollständiger durch die Einführung der alten kleinen Querflöte entsprochen.

Dieselbe hat sich in mehreren Kriegsheeren bis auf den heutigen Tag erhalten, weil sie als der einfachste Repräsentant des melodischen Elementes neben dem rhythmischen, der Wirbeltrommel, sich als außerordentlich wirksam und charakteristisch für die Feldmusik erwiesen hat.

Natürlich blieb man bei dieser einfachen Querflöte nicht lange stehen, sie gab vielmehr nur den ersten Anstoß zur Erfindung und Einführung einer ganzen Reihe anderer Holz-Blasinstrumente, welche wir nach ihren charakteristischen Eigenthümlichkeiten in drei Klassen eintheilen.

Zur ersten zählen:

Die Flöten,

mit einem cylindrisch gebohrten Rohre, welches in drei verschiedene Stücke, — Kopf-, Mittelstück und Fuß — getheilt, und bei welchen der Klang unmittelbar — ohne besonderes Mundstück — hervorgebracht wird.

Hierher gehören: die kleine Querpfeife, die Piccolo-Flöte in verschiedenen Dimensionen, die große Flöte, die Flute d'amour und andere unwesentliche Abarten der Flöte.

In die zweite Klasse fallen:

die Oboen und Fagotts,

Instrumente mit conisch gebohrtem Rohre und einem aus zwei aufeinanderschlagenden Rohrholz-Zungen gebildeten Mundstück.

Hierher zählen: die Oboe, das Englische Horn, das Fagott und das Contrafagott.

Die dritte und letzte Klasse bilden:

die Clarinetten

mit durchweg cylindrisch gebohrtem Rohre und einem aus hartem Holze — schnabelartig — geschnittenen Mundstück, auf dessen abgeschrägte Fläche nur eine einzige Rohrzunge schlägt. Dieses, im Anfange des vorigen Jahrhunderts vom Instrumentenbauer Christoph Denner in Braunschweig erfundene herrliche und außerordentlich umfangreiche Instrument unterscheidet sich außerdem noch dadurch von allen bisher genannten Rohr-Instrumenten, daß es seinen Bruchtheil nicht auf der Octave, sondern auf der Duodecime hat.

Hierher gehören: die kleinen, mittleren und großen Clarinetten in verschiedenen Dimensionen, die Alt-Clarinette, das Bassetthorn und die Baß-Clarinette.

Da die eigenthümliche Klangwirkung dieser drei Klassen von Blasinstrumenten — die Schärfe der kleinen und die Zartheit der großen Flöten, der markige und schneidende Klang der Oboe, der sonore Timbre der Fagotts und der warme, gefällige Schmelz der Clarinette — sich als ganz unentbehrlich für das Ensemble der Militairmusik herausgestellt hat,[1] so ist aber auch streng darauf zu halten, daß dieser charakteristische Reiz der Holz-Blasinstrumente nicht durch ein Uebermaß von Metallzuthaten des Klappenwerkes beeinträchtigt oder wohl ganz beseitigt werde, indem man Holz-Blasinstrumente aus Metall nachzubilden versucht.

§ 5.

Wir wenden und zur Harmonie, dem dritten Factor der Militairmusik, der — wie wir schon früher bemerkten — im Signalhorn seinen Ausdruck findet.

Die Nothwendigkeit, sich bei dem Commando größerer Truppenkörper weitschallender Signale zu bedienen, führte schon im grauen Alterthum zur Erfindung der „Tuba", eines Rohres mit Mund- und Schallstück, das anfänglich in gerader, später — weil handlicher für den Kriegsdienst — in gebogener Form construirt wurde und in solcher, freilich mannigfach modificirter Form[2] noch heute in allen europäischen Kriegsheeren unter dem Namen Signalhorn üblich ist. Bald entstanden neben der alten geraden Tuba des Fußvolkes die sogenannten „Cornua" für die Reiterei, Instrumente, die eine drei- bis viermalige Kreisbiegung des Rohres aufwiesen, späterhin aber sich auf eine zweimalige Biegung beschränkend, im Waldhorn[3] ihre Vollendung und ihren Abschluß fanden.

---

[1] Wir haben die aus der Querpfeife hervorgegangenen Instrumente als vorzugsweise der Melodie dienend bezeichnet, was jedoch nicht ausschließt, daß dieselben im Ensemble ebenso ausgezeichnete Repräsentanten der Harmonie werden können.

[2] Die Orientalen, welche die gebogene Form der Tuba von den Griechen überkamen, veränderten dieselbe, indem sie dem Instrumente die Gestalt des Halbmondes, ihres Nationalzeichens, gaben; von den Russen, die es Flügelhorn nannten, kam die alte Tuba unter mancherlei, für die practische Handhabung günstigeren Abänderungen der Form nach Deutschland.

[3] Dieses herrliche, schon im Mittelalter vorzugsweise zu Jagdsignalen verwendete Instrument wurde von Lully zuerst unter dem Namen Cor de Chasse in die Oper eingeführt.

Eine zweite eigenthümliche Abart der griechischen Tubaform bildete der „Lituus", ein römisches, von Tirtaeus eingeführtes Blasinstrument, welches ein weit längeres Rohr enthielt, in feiner ersten Hälfte cylindrisch und in der zweiten conisch trichterförmig — für die Reiterei aber mit länglicher Kreisbiegung construirt war — das Urbild unserer heut zu Tage sehr vervollkommneten Trompete.

Diese drei Klassen von **Blech-Blasinstrumenten,** das Signalhorn, das Waldhorn und die Trompete bilden — wie sie schon im Alterthum kriegerischen Zwecken dienten und gleichsam zur Waffe gehörten — noch heute das Fundament einer jeden Militairmusik; denn alle die mannigfachen, in neuerer und neuester Zeit erfundenen Instrumente sind, so verschiedenartig und seltsam auch oft deren Namen lauten, in ihrer Construction einzig und allein Abarten jener drei Hauptklassen.

Aus ihnen hat sich naturgemäß eine dreifache Art von Militairmusik gebildet, nämlich:

für die Infanterie-Bataillone:
eine Signalhornmusik,
für die Jäger- und Pionier-Bataillone;
eine Waldhornmusik,
für die Cavallerie- und Artillerie-Regimenter:
eine Trompetenmusik.

Die vielfachen Veränderungen und Modificationen, welche Signalhorn, Waldhorn und Trompete in Bezug auf Form und Structur, im Vergleich zu der alten Tuba, erfahren haben, wurden einmal durch den Wunsch, dem Instrumente, wie wir schon erwähnten, eine handlichere Form zu geben, sodann aber vor Allem durch die Nothwendigkeit herbeigeführt, einen größeren Tonumfang[4] und zugleich eine leichtere Spielbarkeit zu ermöglichen.

Als die bedeutendste Erfindung in Bezug auf eine derartige Erweiterung des Tongebietes für musikalische Zwecke muß die der Ventile bezeichnet werden, die im Jahre 1816 in Preußen gemacht wurde und der Blech-Blasinstrumental-Musik ein ganz neues und weites Feld musikalischer Wirksamkeit erschloß.

---

[4]Gab doch die Tuba recta in den Uranfängen ihres Gebrauches nur zwei Töne her, nämlich den tiefen und dessen nächste Octave.

Wir theilen, wie oben die Holz-Blasinstrumente, so auch die Blech-Blasinstrumente nach ihrer individuellen Construction in drei Klassen. In die erste fallen:

die Signalhörner,

welche ein conisch-kegelförmig konstruirtes, oval gebogenes Rohr, und ein, demselben in sehr verkleinertem Maaßstabe genau nachgebildetes Mundstück besitzen. Zu diesen zählen: das Cornetino, das Sopran-Cornet, das Alt-Cornet, die Bariton- und die Baß-Tuba.

Die zweite Klasse bilden:

die Waldhörner,

denen neben einem längeren, conisch-trichterförmig konstruirten, im Kreise gebogenen und in einem tellerartigen Schallbecher ausmündenden Rohre, ein conische-trichterförmiges Mundstück eigen ist.

Hierher gehören: das Natur-Waldhorn, das Inventions-Waldhorn, das Ventil-Waldhorn, das Sopran- (Wald-) Horn, das Alt- (Wald-) Horn, das Tenor- (Wald-) Horn, das Bariton- (Wald-) Horn, das Baß- (Wald-) Horn und das Contrabaß- (Wald-) Horn.

Die dritte Klasse nehmen ein:

die Trompeten,

deren mittelgroßes, gleichfalls länglich, aber nur einmal gebogenes Rohr, eine cylindrisch conisch-trichterförmige Construktion, dagegen ein kesselförmig gedrechseltes Mundstück aufweist. Hierzu zählen: die Signal-Trompete, die Inventions—Trompete, die Klappen-Trompete, die Zug-Trompete, die Ventil-Trompete; die Zug-Posaune in Alt, Tenor und Baß, welche nach Art der Zug-Trompete durch leichte Verschiebung des Rohres eine vollständige Tonleiter ermöglicht und deshalb aller Ventile entbehren kann; endlich die Tenor- (Ventil-) Trompete, auch Tenorhorn[5] genannnt.

---

[5]Der Verfasser dieser Denkschrift hält, — obschon er selbst in seinen Partituren sich gemwohnheitsmäßig des Ausdruckes Tenorhorn bedient hat — doch den Namen Tenor-Trompete für passender, um jeder Verwechselung mit dem unter den Hörnern aufgeführten kreisförmig gebogenen Tenorhorn vorzubeugen.

§ 6.

Wenn es nun auch den verschiedenen Musikgattungen gestattet bleiben muß, zur Erweiterung ihres Ensembles einzelne Instrumente von einander zu entlehnen, so darf doch dabei in keinem Falle eine Vertauschung der Mundstücke stattfinden, indem die Klangfarbe und der ureigene Charakter eines Instrumentes gerade dadurch bedingt wird, daß es sein ihm eigenthümliches Mundstück behält.

Wir wollen an dieser Stelle noch verschiedener anderer Uebelstände gedenken, die nach unserer besten Ueberzeugung der Militairmusik ganz und gar keinen Vorschub leisten. Hierher gehört vor Allem die durch nichts gerechtfertigte Verwendung der Ventile für die herrliche Zugposaune. Ermöglicht dieselbe doch die größte Gleichmäßigkeit des Klanges in allen Tonlagen und zugleich (vermöge der Züge) eine so reine Intonation, wie sie den Bogeninstrumenten eigen ist. Es wird durch die Ventile auf Kosten des Grund-Charakters der Posaune eine Volubilität ermöglicht, die dem feierlichen Wesen dieses Instrumentes durchaus nicht entspricht.

Ebenso unstatthaft erscheint und die Einführung gewisser Kolosse von Baß-Blasinstrumenten, die in gar keinem Verhältnisse zur menschlichen Gestalt stehen und der Lungenkraft des Spielers geradezu spotten, indem sie fast für jeden einzelnen Ton einen neuen Athemzug erfordern.

Auch sollte der Schallbecher nur bei denjenigen Instrumenten in die Höhe treten, deren Umfang eine handlichere Form nothwendig macht, wie z. B. bei den Fagotts und den Tuben; bei den übrigen Instrumenten aber, mit Ausnahme der Waldhörner — stets nach der Front geradeaus gerichtet bleiben.

§ 7.

Fassen wir nun noch einmal die sämmtlichen Instrumente aller Klassen zusammen, die für die Militair-Musik unentbehrlich erscheinen, so sind dies lauter solche Instrumente, die auch der Kammer-, Orchester- und Opern-Musik angehören, während wir grundsätzlich alle diejenigen Abarten von Instrumenten von der Ausnahme in das Militair-Orchester ausschließen, welche auch die anderen Orchefter-Musiken nicht adoptiren. Denn wir glauben ed wahrlich als eine der schönsten Segnungen der Militair-Musik-Pflege bezeichnen zu dürfen, daß sie gleichsam ein Volks-Instrumental-Lehr-Institut bildet, aus dem sich alle anderen und höheren Zweige der Instrumental-Musik rekrutiren können.

———

Diese hier aufgeführten Instrumente sinden sich, wenn auch unter verschiedenartigen Benennungen und geringen Modificationen, in allen civilisirten Kriegsheeren wieder. So heißt das in Norddeutschland Cornetino genannte Instrument im Süddeutschland Ottavin, dad Sopran-Cornet — Hoch-Flügelhorn, Alt-Cornet — Alt-Flügelhorn, Tenorhorn — Baß-Flügelhorn, Baritontuba — Euphonion, Baßtuba — Bombardon oder Helikon, Contrafagott — Harmoniebaß oder Tritonikon, das Waldhorn kurz Horn; die dort nach der Größe ald kleine, mittlere und große unterschiedenen Clarinetten werden hier nach der Stimmung benannt, und wohl noch Anderes mehr. Die Sache bleibt dieselbe.

Aus allen diesen Instrumenten läßt sich nun recht wohl eine Normal-Besetzung für jede Art der Militair-Musik zusammenstellen, die allen, auch den höchstgestellten Ansprüchen an tonkünstlerische Leistungsfähigkeit genügt.

In dem nachfolgenden Instrumental-Tableau habe ich num den, wie ich glaube, nach vielem Nachdenken und vielen Versuchen gelungenen Versuch gemacht, eine solche Normal-Besetzung aufzustellen.

Anm. In diesen Tabellen bedeutet: Pr. = Primo, Sec. = Secondo, T. = Terzo, Qu. = Quarto.

A. Signalhorn-Musik
für Infanterie-Bataillone und -Regimenter.

Instrument	per Bataillon	per Regiment	Stimmung	Umstimmung
Cornetino	1	3	Es	D
Sopran-Cornet	2 Pr. 1 Sec.	5 Pr. 4 Sec.	B	A
Alt-Cornet	1 Pr. 1 Sec.	3 Pr. 3 Sec.	Es	D
Tenorhorn	1 Pr. 1 Sec.	3 Pr. 3 Sec.	B	A
Baritontuba	1	3		
Baßtuba	1 Pr. 2 Sec.	3 Pr. 2 Sec.		
Zahl der Stimmen u. Mannschaften	12	36		

Bem. Die Cornets (Flügelhörner), Tenorhörner (Baß-Flügelhörner), Bariton- und Baßtuben (Euphonions, Bombardons und Helikons) lassen sich auch durch die in Frankreich, England und Spanien bei der Militair-Musik üblichen sogenannten Saxhörner vertreten.

B. Waldhorn-Musik
für
Jäger- und Pionier-Bataillone.

Instrumente	Hornisten	Signal-Hornisten Verstärkung des Musikcorps	Ins Ganzen	Stimmung	Umstimmung
Cornetino	1	1	2	Es	D
Sopran-Cornet	1 Pr. 1 Sec.	2	4	B	A
Alt-Cornet	1 Pr. 1 Sec.	2	4	Es	D
Tenorhorn	1 Pr. 1 Sec.	2	4	B	A
Baritontuba	1 Pr. 1 Sec.		2	B	A
Baßtuba	1 Pr. 1 Sec.	2	4		
Waldhorn	1 Pr. 1 Sec. 1 T.	3	6	F	E
Trompete	1 Pr. 1 Sec. 1 T.		3	F	E
Zahl der Stimmen u. Mannschaften	17	12	29		

Bem. Für die Waldhorn-Musik ist mit Ausnahme des Cornetino und der Trompete bei allen Instrumenten die Kreisform des Waldhorns gedacht.

C. Trompeten-Musik
für
Cavallerie- und Artillerie-Regimenter.

Instrumente	Cavallerie	Artillerie			Stimmung	Umstimmung
		reitende	zu Fuß	per Regiment zu Fuß		
Cornetino	2	1	1	3	Es	D
Sopran-Cornet	2 Pr. 2 Sec.	2	2	6	B	A
Alt-Cornet	1 Pr. 1 Sec.	2	1	3	Es	D
Tenorhorn	1 Pr. 1 Sec.	2	2	6	B	A
Baritontuba	2	1	1	3		
Baßtuba	2 Pr. 2 Sec.	2	2	6		
Trompete	3 Pr. 2 Sec. 2 T. 2 Qu.	4	4	12	Es	D
Zahl der Stimmen u. Mannschaften	25	14	13	39		

Bem. Bei den Trompeten der Cavallerie und Artillerie muß Die Ventilmaschine schnell und leicht abgenommen und zum Signaldienst ein einfacher Bogen dafür eingesetzt werden können.

D. Janitscharen-Musik
für
Infanterie-Regimenter.

Dieselbe enthält, außer dem Cornetino, auch die sämmtlichen zuvor genannten Blech-Blasinstrumente und setzt sich demnach folgendermaßen zusammen:

Sopran-Cornet 1 Pr. 1 Sec., Alt-Cornet 1 Pr. 1 Sec., Tenorhorn 1 Pr. 1 Sec., Baritontuba 1, Baßtuba 2 Pr. 2 Sec., Waldhorn 1 Pr. 1 Sec., Trompete 1 Pr. 1 Sec. 1 T. 1 Qu., Flöte und zwar kleine und große je 1 Pr. 1 Sec., Oboe 1 Pr. 1 Sec., Kleine Clarinette (As) 1, Mittel-Clarinette (Es) 1 Pr. 1 Sec., Große Clarinette (B) 4 Pr. 4 Sec., Fagott 3, Contrafagott 2, Tenor-Posaune 2, Baß-Posaune 2, Triangel oder Glocken 1, Militairtrommel 2, Becken 1 Paar, Große Trommel 1. In Summa also Stimmen und Musikmannschaften: 46.

Bem. Der Reichthum dieser Instrumentalmusik ermöglicht die getreue Wiedergabe — selbst mit Beibehaltung der Tonart — jeden Orchesterwerkes und macht der leider noch an vielen Orten herrschenden Monotonie, nicht weiter in der Modulation zu schreiten, als es die Es-Stimmung mit ihren nächst verwandten Tonarten zuläßt, ein Ende.

Uebrigens entspricht die Es-Stimmung am meisten dem militairischen Dienste.

Zweiter Theil

Organisation der Musik-Mannschaften

§ 1.

Zahl der Spielleute und Musiker.

Die gesammten Spielleute theilen sich in drei Klassen: Tambours und Hornisten, Trompeter, Hautboisten.
Wir werden nun zunächst jeder Truppengattung die ihr zugehörende Klasse von Spielleuten zuzuweisen haben.
Blicken wir zuerst auf die

Infanterie,

so wird ein Regiment (zu 3 Bataillons, 12 Compagnien = 3000 Mann) folgende Signal-Mannschaften nöthig haben: 1 Stabshornisten und per Bataillon 1 Tambourmajor, 8 Tambours, 12 Hornisten; also per Regiment 63 Mann.
Rechnen wir dazu die Regiments-Kapelle mit 1 Kapellmeister und 46 Hautboisten, so ergiebt dies im Ganzen pro Regiment die Gesammtzahl von 100 Mann.
Ebenso gehören zu einem Jäger- oder Pionier-Bataillon (800 Mann stark): 1 Stabshornist, 17 Hornisten und 12 Signalhornisten, in Summa also 30 Mann.

Wenden wir und nun zur Cavallerie und Artillerie, so sind für jedes

Cavallerie-Regiment

zu 5 Schwadronen gerechnet, pro Schwadron 5 Trompeter erforderlich, per Regiment 1 Stabstrompeter und 25 Trompeter. Endlich bei der

Artillerie

per Regiment a) für die reitende Abtheilung 1 Stabstrompeter und 16 Trompeter; b) für die Artillerie zu Fuß, zu drei Abtheilungen: 1 Stabstrompeter und 39 Trompeter, d. h. per Abtheilung 13 Mann, also im Ganzen 57 Mann.

§ 2.
Anforderungen in Bezug auf die Leistungsfähigkeiten der gesammten Spielleute und Musik-Mannschaften.

1. Der Tambourmajor

muß selbst ein ausgezeichneter Trommelschläger sein, da er die Tambours praktisch, ohne Noten, blos nach dem Gehör, in Ausführung der vorschriftsmäßigen Trommelstreiche zu unterrichten hat.

2. Der Stabshornist des Regiments

hat für die musikalische Ausbildung der Hornisten zu sorgen, indem er ihnen die Handhabung des Instrumentes und die Bildung der Naturtöne auf dem Signalhorne, sodann aber alle diejenigen Elementar-Kenntnisse beizubringen hat, welche zur Ausführung, sowohl der Signale als größerer musikalischer Ausgaben, bei denen ein Theil der Mannschaften später die Tenor- und Baß-Stimmen zu übernehmen hat, nothwendig erscheinen.

Wenn auf der einen Seite die Geschicklichkeit im schnellen Notenlesen für die Märsche und sonstigen musikalischen Vorträge sehr wünschenswerth ist, so gewinnt sie anderseits eine noch viel weittragendere Bedeutung in strategischer Hinsicht, indem die Signale auf Befehl des Feldherrn beliebig verändert werden und sofort zur Verwerthung im Felddienste gelangen können.[6] Mit dem Gewinn dieser Fertigkeit sind die Hornisten zu jeder höheren musikalischen Ausgabe, zu welcher sie der Stabshornist anzuleiten hat, vorbereitet.

Der Stabshornist hat ferner die Hornisten zur Handhabung aller derjenigen chromatischen Blech-Blasinstrumente anzuleiten, welche den verschiedenen Stimmen der Signalhornmusik zugewiesen sind. Denn erst durch die Benutzung der Ventil-Blech-Blasinstrumente wird die Leistungsfähigkeit der Signalhornmusik für den Marsch, den Choral und das Lied, ja sogar für noch höhere musikalische Aufgaben begründet.

Wenn der Stabshornist ein durchgebildeter Tonkünstler und geschickter Elementarlehrer ist, so lassen sich die Mannschaften recht wohl binnen Jahresfrist dahin bringen, eine gute Marschmusik nach Noten zu executiren.

Nach Ablauf seiner Militair-Dienstzeit wird aber gewiß jeder Hornist, der darüber hinaus capitulirt und bei der Musik bleiben will, die Reife zum Hautboisten oder Trompeter gewonnen haben.

Hieraus erhellt, von welcher Wichtigkeit die Pflege der Signalhornmusik sein muß, da sie recht eigentlich eine Vorschule und das sicherste Rekrutirungs-Mittel für das ganze Militair-Musikwesen einer Armee bildet.

Die Organisation der Signalhornmusik in der Königlich Preußischen Armee wurde von dem Verfasser dieser Denkschrift chon 1837 in's Leben gerufen.

Ihr haben wir es zu danken, daß im Jahre 1861 binnen 6 Monaten 32 Hornmusik-Chöre a 22 Mann und 10 Trompeter-Chöre a 16 Mann für die neuformirten Regimenter errichtet werden konnten.

Ist es nicht charakteristisch, daß, während man gegenwärtig in anderen großstaatischen Armeen wegen mangelnder Musik—Mannschaften bei der Cavallerie, der Artillerie, ja sogar bei den Jäger-Bataillonen die Musikcorps gänzlich aufzulösen gezwungen ist, in der Königlich Preußischen Armee die Militairmusik bei allen Truppentheilen in vollster Blüthe steht?

---

[6]Diese Fähigkeit, fließend vom Blatte zu spielen, ist den Cavallerie-Trompetern der Königlich Preußischen Armee ohne Ausnahme eigen.

3. Der Regiments-Kapellmeister

muß nicht allein vorzügliche musikalische Bildung und Kenntnisse des gesammten Instrumental-Wesens besitzen, sondern auch in vielen militairischen Angelegenheiten erfahren sein.

Von ihm verlangt man die Kenntniß der im Exercier- Reglement vorgeschriebenen Tambourstreiche, Signale, Märsche der Trommeln im Ensemble mit den Querflöten, des Zapfenstreiches, der Cadenzen des Präsentir- und des Defilir-Marsches, damit er im Stande ist, darüber zu wachen, daß sich nicht fehlerhafte Auffassungen der Notation einschleichen. Er ist die oberste musikalische Autorität im Regimente, der sich der Stabshornist, die Tambourmajors, sowie sämmtliche Signalmannschaften und Hautboisten zu fügen haben. Der Regiments-Kapellmeister hat deshalb auch seine Aufmerksamkeit auf die musikalische Ausbildung der Hornisten zu richten, den Musikunterricht nach einem bestimmten Lehrplane zu ordnen und zu beauffichtigen, beim Ankauf der Instrumente und Musikalien sein gewissenhaftes Urtheil abzugeben und endlich die Regiments-Kapelle in ihrer Leistungsfähigkeit zur möglichst höchsten Stufe tonkünstlerischer Tüchtigkeit zu geleiten.

Allerdings muß einem Manne, dem so vielseitige Thätigkeit zugemuthet, eine so große Verantwortlichkeit aufgebürdet wird, jedenfalls ein höherer Dienstgrad zugetheilt werden, als der eines Unterofficiers.

4. Die Hautboisten

müssen ohne Ausnahme praktisch durchgebildete Musiker sein und besonders das ihnen im Corps zugewiesene Instrument fertig zu spielen verstehen.

Außerdem muß man bei ihnen auch noch die Behandlung irgend eines Saiten-Instrumentes voraussetzen, indem dem Regiments-Kapellmeister heutzutage aller Orten auch die Pflege der Kammer-, Salon- und Tanz-Orchester-Musik obliegt.

Abgesehen von dem oft sehr ergiebigen Musikerwerb verleiht solche Pflege des Streich-Orchesters der Regiments-Kapelle ein höheres Ansehen in den Augen der Kunstkenner und übt vor Allem einen mächtigen Einfluß auf die Bildung des guten Geschmackes und Musiksinnes der Einwohnerschaft in den betreffenden Garnisonen aus.

5. Der Stabshornist für die Jäger- und Pionier- Waldhornmusik

hat — wie der Stabshornist bei der Infanterie — eine theoretische Durchbildung in der Tonkunst nachzuweisen. Ihm fällt auch die musikalische Ausbildung der Signalmannschaften anheim, wobei er sich der sehr wesentlichen Mithülfe seiner Hornisten bedienen mag.

6. Die Hornisten der Waldhornmusik

müssen das ihnen im Corps zugewiesene Blech-Blasinstrument ganz fertig zu spielen verstehen und im Primavista-Spiel ausgebildet sein, außerdem — wie wir schon bei den Hautboisten der Infanterie voraussetzen — auch Uebung in der Behandlung irgend eines Saiteninstrumentes haben, damit der Stabshornist im Stande ist, aus seinen 17 gelernten Musikern eine leidliche Streich-Instrumental-Musik zu organisiren.

An die Jäger- und Pionier-Musik, welche sich außer den Waldhörnern und Trompeten noch der Unterstützung von 17 Fachmusikern erfreut, müssen natürlich viel höhere tonkünstlerische Ansprüche gestellt werden können, als an die Signalhornmusik.

7. Der Stabstrompeter

Wohl an keinen Militair-Musiker werden größere Ansprüche in Bezug auf die Doppeltüchtigkeit des Soldaten wie des Tonkünstlers gestellt, als an den Stabstrompeter des Regimentes. Er soll in allen Cavallerie-Dienstzweigen vollständig zu Hause sein und in der Wiedergabe der Signale zu Fuß wie zu Pferde das Vorzüglichste leisten.

Darf man wohl nun annehmen, daß er eine treffliche Ausbildung in der Tonkunst, sowohl als ausübender Spieler seines Instrumentes, wie auch als Arrangeur für das Ensemble seines Trompeter-Corps beim Eintritt in seine Stellung besitzen muß, so wird gleichwohl die andere Seite seiner Berufsthätigkeit, die des strengen und tüchtigen Soldaten, erst in mehrjähriger praktischer Dienststellung gewonnen werden können. Deshalb ist die Charge des Stabstrompeters immer aus den Reihen der Trompeter heranzubilden und zu ergänzen.

Von der hervorragendsten Bedeutung ist seine Thätigkeit im Felddienste. Er darf vor der Front des Regimentes seinen Commandeur keinen Augenblick verlassen, muß, ihm zur Seite reitend, alle seine Commandos richtig auffassen, das betreffende Signal mit Blitzesschnelle erschallen und alsdann durch die, in die Schwadronen einrangirten Trompeter über das ganze Regiment verbreiten lassen.

Dem Tode kühn in's Auge schauend, darf er sich durch Nichts zerstreuen lassen, da der geringste Fehler, das kleinste Mißverständniß hier die unberechenbarsten Folgen zum Nachtheile des Ganzen herbeiführen würde.

So streng der Stabstrompeter als Soldat vor der Front des Regimentes erscheint, eben so milde hat er seinen Trompetern als Musikmeister gegenüber zu treten.

Die ausübende Tonkunst kann nur unter mildem Regimente gedeihen; nicht militairische Gewalt, sondern gründliche Belehrung vermag diejenige Liebe und Begeisterung für (Ensemble-) Musik zu erwecken, ohne welche die ausübenden Musiker immer nur den Stempel musikalischer Dressur tragen würden.

Dem Stabstrompeter der Artillerie zu Fuß stehen zur Organisation seiner Musik 39 Signalmannschaften zur Disposition, welche er so einzutheilen und in ihren Stimmen zu besetzen hat, daß jede Abtheilung des Regimentes mit ihren 13 Mann zugleich eine vollständige Trompetenmusik gewinnt. Es liegt auf der Hand, daß diese drei Abtheilungen in der Stimmenbesetzung genau übereinstimmen müssen, damit sie beim Zusammenschluß des Regimentes — ohne jede Vorbereitung — ein großes Ensemble zu formiren im Stande sind.

Demgemäß hat auch der Stabstrompeter seine Arrangements einzurichten und dafür zu sorgen, daß auch bei Trennung der Abtheilungen in verschiedene Garnisonen nach gleichen Prinzipien verfahren werde. Ihm wird es auch anheimfallen, dem Regiments-Kommando für die Führung der 2. und 3. Abtheilung geeignete Trompeter in Vorschlag zu bringen.

8. Der Trompeter

bei der Kavallerie und Artillerie hat schon bei seinem Eintritt in's Regiment Proben musikalischer Tüchtigkeit auf irgend einem, der Trompetenmusik zugehörenden Instrumente, sowie im Primavistaspiel abzulegen.

Die Erlernung der Trompetensignale darf ihm daher selbst überlassen bleiben. Er wird dazu außer einigen Winken des Stabstrompeters keiner weiteren Instruktion, als der Vorlage der Notation des Exerzier-Reglements bedürfen.

Auch für den Trompeter erscheint die Ausübung irgend eines Streich- oder Holz-Blasinstrumentes sehr wünschenswerth, damit neben der Blechmusik auch noch ein Orchester mit Saiteninstrumenten zur Ausführung von Salon- und Tanzmusiken hergestellt werden kann, welches dem Offiziercorps, wie den Bewohnern des betreffenden Garnisonortes Genuß, den Trompetern aber einen oft recht bedeutenden Privaterwerb gewähren wird.

Bei den Kavallerie- und Artillerieregimentern können, außer den erforderlichen Signalmannschaften, besondere Musikcorps nicht beritten gemacht werden, deshalb müssen die Signaltrompeter also gleichfalls den Soldaten und Musiker in einer Person vereinigen. Da nun die soldatische Ausbildung — das Fußexerciren, der Wachtdienst, die Instruktionsstunden, sodann die Erlernung des Reitens, Fechtens, Schießens — geraume Zeit erfordert und nur im praktischen Dienste beim Regimente gewonnen werden kann, bleibt für einen gründlichen Musikunterricht bei den Signaltrompetern — wie er bei der Infanterie möglich wurde — durchaus keine Zeit übrig, zumal die Kavalleriemusik im Besitze viel reicherer Instrumentalmittel ist, als eine Signalhornmusik und deshalb auf einer weit höheren Kunststufe steht.

Mithin ist es unerläßlich, bei Organisation dieser Musikgattung praktisch geschulte Musiker anzuwerben, und da, wo solche mangeln, selbst kleine Opfer an Funktionszulagen nicht zu scheuen.

§ 3.

Die Centralisation der Armee-Musik

hat der Verfasser seit langen Jahren erstrebt und durch endliche Herstellung der, dieser Denkschrift beigegebenen obigen Instrumentaltableaus gewonnen — natürlich unter der Voraussetzung, daß von der darin vorgeschriebenen Stimmenbesetzung bei allen Truppentheilen der Armee eben so wenig als von den anderen kriegsministeriellen Bestimmungen abgewichen werden darf.

Die Aufgabe, solche Centralisation der Armeemusik nach allen Richtungen hin durchzuführen, zu leiten und zu überwachen, würde aber einem tonkünstlerischen Oberhaupte von umfassendster Fachkenntniß, einem vom Kriegsministerium ressortirenden Armee-Kapellmeister zugetheilt werden müssen, denn gleichwie durch Vorlage der Notation im Exercierreglement das Signalwesen centralisirt ist, kann dies auch mit der gesammten Armeemusik geschehen, wenn alle Märsche, Choräle, Hymnen rc. nach Vorschrift des Instrumentaltableaus instrumentirt und in der dort vorgezeichneten Stimmenbesetzung in einer und derselben Partitur von der Centralstelle aus sämmtlichen Truppenkommandos auf dem Wege mechanischer Vervielfältigung zugänglich gemacht werden.

So wird es nicht allein jedem einzelnen Musikcorps ermöglicht, ein Tonstück nach Vorschrift mustergültig zu spielen, sondern es können auch mehrere, ja viele Musikcorps der verschiedensten Musikgattungen, zu kleineren, größeren, ja riesenmäßig verstärkten Ensembles vereinigt, ohne jegliche Vorbereitung dasselbe Musikstück gemeinsam exekutiren.[7]

Da vom Kriegsministerium aus nicht allein alle Bestimmungen über die Etatsverhältnisse, die Pensionsansprüche für die verschiedenen Chargen der Spielleute und Musiker in der Armee, sondern auch die Vorschriften über die Herausgabe der Signale, der Armeemärsche, sowie aller anderen für die Armeemusik zu bestimmenden Tonstücke ergehen, so wird es zur unerläßlichen Bedingung werden, das Gesammtfeld des Armee-Musikwesens einer Abtheilung im Kriegsministerium zu überweisen, von welcher unter dem Beisitze des Armee-Kapellmeisters alle hierher gehörigen Angelegenheiten, sowie ganz besonders die Anstellung der militairmusikalischen Corpsführer — wohl das wichtigste Element der Militairmusik — überwacht werden muß.

Gleichwie dem Gemeinen, welcher über seine Dienstzeit hinaus im Heere verbleiben will, ein Avancement zum Gefreiten, Unteroffizier, Feldwebel oder Wachtmeister, ja sogar, wenn er die Kenntnisse besitzt, noch ein höherer Grad, z. B. der eines Zahlmeisters in Aussicht gestellt ist, so müßte man in gleicher Weise ein entsprechendes Avancement für die Musikmannschaften nämlich vom Tambour oder Hornisten als Gemeiner, zum musikalischen Hornisten als Gefreiter, von diesem zum Hautboisten oder Trompeter als Unteroffizier,

---

[7] Aufgaben dieser Art im Musikwesen bieten in der Königlich Preuß. Armee keine Schwierigkeiten, und es haben — Dank solcher Centralisation — in derselben schon oft Ensemble-Musik-Aufführungen von mehr denn 1000 Musikern stattgefunden.

von diesem zum Stabshornisten, Stabshautboisten oder Stabstrompeter als Feldwebel oder Wachtmeister, endlich von letzterem Grade zum Regiments-Kapellmeister mit dem Range eines Regiments-Zahlmeisters stattfinden.

Wenn somit angenommen wird, daß die Musikdirigenten-Aspiranten nur aus den Hautboisten oder Trompetern hervorgehen dürfen, so wird es als eine besondere Belohnung für treu geleistete Militairdienste angesehen werden, wenn das Kriegsministerium die bravsten, tüchtigsten, in jeder militairischen Tugend bewährten Musikmannschaften Behufs höherer Ausbildung in der Tonkunst einem Konservatorium überweist, von wo aus sie alsdann — unter gleichzeitigem Dienstavancement — wieder in die Armee zurücktreten.

Dies wären die Grundzüge, nach welchen eine schulgerecht gebildete Armeemusik organisirt werden muß.

Sollten dieselben allgemein Wurzeln schlagen, sollte für die Militairmusik, (welche als ein eigener, selbstständiger Instrumentalzweig der Tonkunst in allen gebildeten Kriegsheeren anerkannt wird) namentlich durch allgemeine Einführung meiner Instrumentaltableaus, eine ebenso unerschütterliche Basis gewonnen werden, als selbige der Kammer-Orchestermusik bereits eigen ist, — deren Instrumentalmittel allgemein anerkannt und für die ganze Musikwelt als sanktionirt gelten — so wäre dies wahrlich der höchste Lohn für mein vierzigjähriges treues und begeistertes Wirken auf diesem Felde der Tonkunst.

Berlin, den 6. November 1868.

W. Wieprecht,
Direktor der gesammten Musik des Gardecorps

Anhang

Bericht Wieprecht's über den Sieg der Musik der preußischen Garde bei dent internationalen Wettkampf der europäischen Militärmusik auf der Pariser Weltausstellung.

Am Sonntag, den 21. Juli 1867, war der internationale Wettkampf im Industriepalast. Schon früh um 10 Uhr machte sich vor der Kaserne, in welcher wir lagen, ein Wogen und Drängen des schaulustigen Publikums bemerkbar; die Pariser wollten die fremden Musikcorps in ihrer parademäßigen Uniform nach dem Bestimmungsorte ausrücken sehen.

Der Saal des Wettkampfes bildete ein längliches Viereck, in dessen Mitte dekorirte Bänke für die sämmtlichen Musikcorps ausgestellt waren. Diese Plätze waren umschlossen von einem duflenden Blumenflor der schönsten Gewächse, hinter welchen sich eine terrassenartige, breite Passage befand. Von dieser Passage aus breiteten sich die Logen der Zuhörer terrassenartig bis an die beiden Enden des mit entsprechenden Emblemen und Wappen geschmückten Saales. An einem Ende desselben befanden sich die kaiserlichen Hoflogen, an welche sich von beiden Seiten die Logen der höchsten Staatsbeamten und Gesandtschaften anschlossen. Vor diesen Logen befand sich ein großer Tisch für die Jury, mit den erforderlichen Schreibmaterialien versehen. In kurzer Distanz, unmittelbar vor der Jury, war die Orchestertribüne in angemessener Höhe aufgebaut. Am andern Ende des Saales befand sich ein großes logenartiges Plateau als Versammlungsort der gesammten Musikcorps. Die letztern ordneten sich hier nach vorhergegangener Losung zum Abmarsch auf die für sie bestimmten Bänke.

Nr. 1. Das Badenser Musikcorps, unter Leitung seines Kapellmeisters Burg (54 Musiker). Nr. 2. Erstes Regiment vom spanischen Geniecorps, unter Führung seines Kapellmeisters Moimo (64 Musiker). Nr. 3. Musikcorps der preußischen Garde, unter Führung ihrer Musikmeister Meinberg und Saro und deren Chef Wieprecht (85 Musiker). Wir hatten an Holzblasinstrumenten 4 Flöten, 4 Oboen, 6 Fagotts, 4 Kontrafagotts, 1 kleines Fagott, 4 Mittelfagotts, 16 große Klarinetten. Wir verfügten an Blechblasinstrumenten über 4 Sopran-Cornetts, 4 Alt-Cornetts, 4 Waldhörner, 4 Tenorhörner, 2 Bariton-Tuben, 6 Baß-Tuben, 8 Trompeten, 8 Zug-Posaunen. An Schlag-Instrumenten hatten wir 2 kleine Trommeln, 1 große Trommel, 2 Paar Becken, 1 Glockenspiel nebst Triangel, in Summa 85 Instrumente. Nr. 4. Das österreichische Regiment Herzog von Würtemberg Nr. 73 unter dem Kapellmeister Zimmermann (76 Musiker). Nr. 5. Das belgische Grenadierregiment, unter dem Kapellmeister C. Benner (59 Musiker). Nr. 6. Das baierische erste Infanterieregiment unter seinem Kapellmeister Siebenkaes (51 Musiker). Nr. 7. Holländische Grenadier- und Chasseurregimenter, unter dem. K.-M. Duntler (56 Musiker). No. 8. Die russische Chevalier-Garde unter Führung des Corps-Kapellmeisters Doerfelt (71 Mann). Nr. 9. Französische Garde, à guide de la garde Imperiale, Chef Cressonois (62 Musiker). Nr. 10. Garde de Paris, Chef Paulus (56 Musiker).

Die Corps nahmen ihren Marsch vom Plateau herab in das Parterre des Saales in der genannten Reihenfolge, in welcher Ordnung sie auf den bestimmten Plätzen sich niederließen. Die Badenser bestiegen zunächst die Musiktribüne und begannen mit dem Adagio der Oberon-Ouvertüre. Die Musiker, trotzdem sie alle ihre Instrumente angesetzt hatten, wurden indeß vom Publikum nicht gehört. 40000 Zuhörer blickten mit gespannter Aufmerksamkeit nach den Musikern, deren technische Gestikulationen sie zwar bemerkten, deren Töne sie aber nicht vernehmen konnten. Ein allgemeines Murren erfolgte, ein tumultuarischer Lärm, klopfend und schreiend: „Wir hören keine Musik! die Musik in die Mitte des Saales!" Der letztere Wunsch war indeß vorläufig unausführbar. Die Musiker schlossen mit dem Adagio der Ouvertüre ab und spielten statt derselben das Finale aus der Loreley von Mendelssohn, welches mehr auf einer Ensemblewirkung ruhte, als das Adagio der Oberon-Ouvertüre, unter fortdauerndem Lärmen und Pochen bis zu Ende. Hieran schloß sich der Vortrag der Oberon-Ouvertüre, welche aber unter dem ununterbrochenen Lärmen des Publikums ganz spurlos vorüberging. Dem aufmerksamen Hörer konnte indeß nicht unbemerkt bleiben, daß dieses Musikcorps sehr tüchtige musikalisch gebildete Kräfte besitze, die unter günstigeren Verhältnissen sicherlich ihre wohlverdiente Anerkennung gefunden haben würden.

Unter solchen mißlichen Umständen betraten die Spanier die Musiktribüne und begannen eine Phantasie über spanische Nationallieder, woran sich die Konkurrenzaufgabe anschloß. Auch diese Musik verschwand spurlos unter fortdauernder Unruhe und lauter Unzufriedenheit des Publikums.

Mir war nicht entgangen, daß die Musikcorps den Zweck ihrer Aufgabe ganz irrthümlich aufgefaßt hatten und in der Meinung, hier ein großes Militairkonzert ausführen zu sollen, das Ziel, vor einer Jury zu spielen, durchaus verwechselten. Statt Front zu nehmen zur Jury, nahmen sie diese zum Publikum. Die Länge des Saales bereitete hierdurch nicht allein einen Widerhall, sondern ein komplettes Echo von mindestens der Mensur um eine ganze Viertelnote des Taktes. Wir nahmen deshalb bei unserer Ausstellung Front zur Jury, ich allein als Dirigent nahm Front zum Publikum; der Klang unserer Instrumente gewann hierdurch eine ganz kurze Distanz. War doch der Zweck dieses ganzen Conkurses die Prüfung der Militairmusik und nicht der eines Militairkonzertes vor einem 40000 köpfigen Publikum, wozu mindestens taufend Musiker gehörten, um dem letztern Zwecke zu entsprechen.

Wir begannen mit meiner Prophetenphantasie, die genau auf die Klangwirkung einer Militairmusik berechnet ist. Schon durch eine andere Ausstellung zogen wir die Aufmerksamkeit des Publikums auf uns und es trat eine allmähliche Ruhe unter dem letztern ein. Noch günstiger gestaltete sich der Moment für uns in dem starken Unisono aller Instrumente, womit meine Phantasie beginnt, welche sich schon im 7. Takte in eine im rechten fortissimo erklingende Harmonie verläuft. Hier ergriff das Publikum von allen Seiten ein zusammenhängender musikalischer Effekt und von allen Seiten erschallten die Worte: „Silence, silence, quelle belle musique"! (Still, still, welch' eine schöne Musik!) Es trat eine große Ruhe ein, unter welcher jede, ja die feinste Nüance der Spieler zu Gehör gebracht werden konnte. Vor dem Schlußsatze der Phantasie wurde mein Solo-Cornetist für die Ausführung seiner vorgeschriebenen Cadenz durch einen nicht enden wollenden Applaus belohnt, und ich besürchtete fast, daß die gewünschte Ruhe nicht wieder eintreten und unsere Musik um den schönsten Lorbeer gebracht werden könnte. Indeß merkte doch das Publikum wohl aus meinen Verneigungen, daß das Musikstück noch nicht geendet habe; man wurde ruhiger, sodaß wir die Phantasie bei ganz außerordentlicher Stille im Saal glücklich zu Ende führen konnten.

Jetzt ging es zur Hauptaufgabe des Conkurses, nämlich zur Ausführung der Oberon-Ouvertüre. Die musikalische Intelligenz unserer Hautboisten hatte von selbst verstanden, daß in diesem ungeheuren Raume durch die vorgeschriebenen Pianostellen des Adagios nichts erreicht werden könne; auf meinen Wink wurden hier nächstdem die Pianos, welche ich mit gedämpften Instrumenten zu exekutiren vorbereitet hatte, fistirt. Das Allegro der Ouvertüre wurde sehr feurig und in sehr lebhaftem Tempo vorgetragen. Ein nicht enden wollender Beifall von allen Seiten, den selbst die Herren der Jury durch Erhebung von ihren Plätzen kundgaben, begleitete diesen unsern Vortrag bei seinem Schlusse.

Froh und wohlgemuth traten wir von der Tribüne an unsere alten Plätze und nun folgten die Oesterreicher, deren kolossale Baßinstrumente, die ungeheuren Bombardons, Helikons u.s.w. uns einen gewaltigen Schreck einjagten, um so mehr, als eine vorherrschende Zuneigung die Oesterreicher begünstigte. Sie nahmen, wohl fühlend die fehlerhafte Aufstellung der Spanier u.s.w., dieselbe Position, wie wir sie in veränderter Weise genommen hatten; sie begannen mit der Rossini'schen Tell-Ouvertüre. Wenn auch nicht geleugnet werden kann, daß Intonation und Ensemble den tonkünstlerischen Anforderungen genügten, so war dies doch nicht in Hinsicht auf die musikalische Auffassung der Fall. Das schöne Solo des englischen Horns im Andante pastorale wurde auf einem Flügelhorn exekutirt. Die österreichische Musik führt weder Hautboen noch Fagott und war mithin auf diesen musikalischen Mißgriff hingewiesen. Die Verbindung beider Soli des englischen Horns mit der Flöte war, da das erstere nothgedrungen auf einem Flügelhorn exekutirt werden mußte, eine nicht passende, wenigstens in Paris, wo der Komponist lebt und seine Gegenwart im Conzerte angenommen werden durfte. Ebenso stand auch der Klang der Instrumente nicht im Vergleich mit ihren unnatürlichen Kolossen. Das Ganze hatte eine etwas gedämpfte und bis zum Extrem kurz abgerissene Klangwirkung. In der Ausführung von Tänzen und Defilirmärschen, Potpourri's u. s. w. haben die Oesterreicher eine Meisterschaft erreicht, wie wohl keines der anderen anwesenden Musikcorps. Was darüber hinausgeht, namentlich klassische Musik, wird, gleichwie die Tanzmusik, in allen Situationen auf das kürzeste Stackato basirt. Im Uebrigen ist ihre Militairmusik charakteristisch und ihrem Zweck entsprechend. Auch die Oesterreicher wurden mit vielem Beifall Seitens des Publikums beglückt.

Jetzt traten die Belgier hervor, — wunderbarer Weise, wie die Baiern und Holländer mit großen Streichkontrabässen und Kesselpauken ausgerüstet. Sie begannen mit einer Phantasie über Themata der Oper „Tell", deren Schlußsatz das Allegro der Tell-Ouvertüre bildete. Das Publikum hatte also das Vergnügen, die Tell-, sowie die Oberon-Ouvertüre zweimal hintereinander zu genießen. Die belgische Militairmusik, welche ich vor 25 Jahren kennen gelernt und deren Konkurrenz mir am gefährlichsten erschien, ging hier sonderbarer Weise bedeutungslos vorüber, obwohl mir bekannt, daß ihre Hautboisten insgesammt durchgebildete Musiker sind; es fehlte derselben der militairische Charakter, den sie ganz aus den Augen verlor, was durch die Verwendung von Streichinstrumenten und Kesselpauken seine Begründung findet.

Die Baiern schlossen sich hieran mit einer Phantasie über Heimathslüfte, die das Längenmaß sehr überschritt, so daß sich im Publikum gleich wieder die erforderliche Ruhe verlor. Die Oberon-Ouvertüre wurde nicht mit der Delikatesse und dem poetischen Ergusse vorgetragen, wie es das Werk erfordert.

Die Holländer folgten jetzt mit dem Vortrage einer Phantasie über Themata aus Gounod's Faust. Die Aufmerksamkeit des Publikums für den Gegenstand hatte sich hier schon dermaßen abgeschwächt, daß deren Leistungsfähigkeit nicht diejenige Anerkennung fand, die sie wohl verdiente; überhaupt waren die Tonstücke nach freier Wahl im Zeitmaaße alle zu lang gehalten.

Jetzt traten die Russen hervor. Ihr Aeußeres, was Bekleidung und Dekorirung mit ihren geharnischten Helmen anbelangt, machte eine imposante Wirkung und frischte das Interesse des Publikums einigermaßen wieder auf. Sie spielten nach freier Wahl eine Phantasie: „Lebens-Ouvertüre für den Kaiser" von Glinka. Diese Ouvertüre hatte mehr die Form einer Phantasie über russische Nationallieder. Sie wurden in echt nationaler Weise wundervoll vorgetragen. Die Gesammtwirkung dieser Musik war militairisch charakteristisch, obgleich der Vortrag ihrer Musikpiecen mehr Wärme hätte ausdrücken können. Namentlich darf dies von der Oberon-Ouvertüre gesagt werden, welche auch in einem überaus langsamen Tempo exekutirt wurde. Die Leistungsfähigkeit dieses Musikcorps überraschte in der That um so mehr, als die allgemeine Meinung herrschte, daß die Russen in der Instrumental-Tonkunst noch nicht soweit vorgeschritten seien, als andere Nationen.

Endlich erschien der Moment, wo die Erfindungen des Instrumentenmachers Sax bei diesem Konkurse ihre Sanktion vor der ganzen Welt erhalten sollten. Es traten als Repräsentanten dieser Erfindungen die beiden Corps: „Guide de la garde Imperiale": und „Garde de Paris" auf. Das erste Corps spielte eine geistreich komponirte Phantasie über den „Carneval von Venedig" von Charles Collin. Diese Phantasie enthielt höchst interessante Instrumentaleffekte, die mit einer außerordentlichen Virtuosität exekutirt wurden. Das Ganze war in einem höchst humoristischen Style gehalten, so daß man dies Musikstück sehr gut als — Phantasie-Burleske bezeichnen könnte. Der Charakter der Militairmusik aber lag dieser Musik sehr fern, so daß man behaupten möchte, die Militairmusik sei hier schon vollständig im Virtuosenthum aufgegangen. Dergleichen gehört mehr in einen Salon, als vor die Front eines Regimentes.

Das zweite Musikcorps trug ebenfalls nach freier Wahl Chor und Marsch und die Einleitung aus der Oper Lohengrin vor. Chor und Marsch machten eine schöne Wirkung. Die Einleitung, die der Komponist mit lauter Sordinen im Orchester vorgeschrieben hat, und welche von den Saxophons (Blechklarinetten) so zu sagen gesäuselt wurde, war auch wohl nicht geeignet, eine Militairmusik zu veranschaulichen. Wenn auch die außerordentliche Virtuosität und Präcision, mit der diese Tonstücke vorgetragen wurden, nicht zu verkennen ist, so fordert eine Musik, die des Kriegers Muth für Kampf und Sieg anfeuern soll, solche Mittel nicht.

Es war wohl sehr natürlich, daß nach einer 5 stündigen Aufführung, in der man zehnmal gezwungen war, die Oberon-Ouvertüre mit anzuhören, eine Abspannung der Zuhörer sich geltend machte. Es ist dies eben der Grund oder die verfehlte Richtung, welcher die französische Militairmusik seit 25 Jahren huldigt, daß die Leistungsfähigkeit ihrer eigenen Landsmannshaften nicht mehr so zu enthusiasmiren vermochte, als es den Preußen und Oesterreichern geglückt war. Ueberhaupt ist es in den letzten drei Decennien zur Maxime geworden, von Industriellen die Werkzeuge der Militairmusik zu dem Vortheil der letztern ausbeuten zu lassen. Die Orchester-Kammermusik besitzt in ihrer Harmonie der Flöten, Hautboen, der Fagotts, der Klarinetten, Waldhörner und der Posaunen, diese so vortrefflich sich für die Militairmusik eignenden Werkzeuge, die mit Hinzuziehung der modernen chromatischen Blechinstrumente, z. B. der Kornetts in Sopran und Alt, der Tenorhörner, der Bariton und Baßtuben, endlich mit Zunahme der üblichen Schlagwerkzeuge ein so unendlich reiches und schönes Material für die Militairmusik bilden, daß es all dergleichen Erfindungen, die doch nur alle Abarten jener sind, nicht bedarf, um eine charakteristische und kräftig klingende Militairmusik herzustellen.

Das letzte Musikcorps verließ um 6 1/2 Uhr die Musiktribüne. Alles, Publikum und Musiker, harrten in gespannter Erwartung der Entscheidung. In diesem Moment trat der kgl. pr. Konsul, Herr Bamberger, Mitglied der Jury, freudig erregt zum preußischen Musikcorps heran, uns verkündend, daß wir nach dem Ausspruch der Jury den ersten großen Preis errungen hätten. Gleichzeitig trat auch der Sekretair des Konkurs-Komitee's, Herr Jonas, am mich mit der Aufforderung heran, mit ihm zum General Mellenet zu gehen. Wir mußten unsern Gang über die Musiktribüne nehmen, um zur Jury zu gelangen. Als wir Beide daselbst anlangten, waren sämmtliche Mitglieder der Jury verschwunden; sie hatten sich in ein anstoßendes Kabinet zu einer zweiten Berathung zurückgezogen. Herr Jonas war über dieses Verschwinden der Jury erstaunt und bat mich, einen Moment zu warten und den Platz nicht zu verlassen, damit er mich wiederfinden könne. Ich folgte seiner Aufforderung, doch leider umsonst. Nach einer guten halben Stunde, in welcher das Publikum schon des langen Harrens auf Verkündigung des Resultates ungeduldig geworden war, erschienen in der Mitte des Saales auf einem Balkon die Mitglieder des Komitees und General Mellenet meldete Folgendes: Die Jury habe sich aus gewissen Gründen veranlaßt gefühlt, vom alten Programm dahin abzuweichen, daß aus dem einen großen Preise, zu welchem 2000 Francs zugelegt wurden, 3 große Preise à 2500 Francs, ein zweiter Preis aus jenen zugelegten 2000 Francs, endlich noch ein dritter Preis per 1000 Francs bestimmt worden sei. Er bezeichne die ersten 3 großen Preise nach alphabetischer Ordnung, um keinem der Gewinner den Vorzug zu geben. 1. pour les Autrichiens; 2. pour les Français; 3. pour les Prussiens; für die Russen den Preis der Zulage per 2000 Francs; für die Holländer den Preis per 1000 Francs. So endete dieser denkwürdige Konkurs, aus welchem die Preußen allein als Sieger hervorgehen mußten.

Am 30. (Dienstag) fand eine Marschaufführung vor Sr. Majestät dem Kaiser und der ganzen Suite in dem Tuilleriengarten, Abends 5 Uhr, statt. Nach Beendigung derselben mußten die gesammten Musikcorps ein geschlossenes Carré bilden. Seine Majestät nebst Suite vertheilten hierbei eigenhändig Orden an die kommandirten fremden Offiziere, sowie an sämmtliche anwesenden Regiments-Kapellmeister. Hier hatte ich die Ehre, das Ritterkreuz der Ehrenlegion aus der Hand des Kaisers unter der schmeichelhaftesten Anerkennung meiner Verdienste im Gebiete der Militairmusik zu empfangen. Die Corps und alle Anwesenden brachten dem Kaiser ein dreimaliges donnerndes Hurrah. Das Carré trat wieder in Linie und die Musikcorps begannen ihren Abmarsch. Mich beglückte an diesem Abend eine Einladung zur kaiserlichen Tafel, bei welcher Gelegenheit der Kaiser sich mit mir lange über das Wesen der Militairmusik unterhielt, viele Fragen an mich richtete und das Bedauern ausdrückte, daß er alles das, was ich ihm über diesen Gegenstand vorgetragen, nicht als Schriftstück besitze. Beim Abschiede gab ich das Versprechen, über die militairmusikalische Organisation eines Kriegsheeres eine Denkschrift zu verfassen. (Diese Denkschrift ist unsern Lesern ja jetzt bekannt.)

Part II

English

Preface

THE FOLLOWING MEMORANDUM comes from the legacy of the well-known former director of all the music of the Prussian Guard Corps, W. Wieprecht, who died in Berlin on 4 August 1872. It was his last work. Not long before his death, he handed it over to the writer Mr Friedrich Bücker, who had written Wieprecht's biography for *Daheim* a few years earlier, with the request that it be published at a suitable time, without any restrictions. He told Mr Bücker that the memoir was the fulfillment of a promise he had made to Emperor Napoleon III of France after the victory of the music of the Prussian Guards in Paris, when the Emperor presented him with the Order of the Legion of Honour and invited him to the table. He promised the Emperor that he would write a detailed memorandum on the purposes and organization of army music, kept his promise and intended to present the document in person in Paris. However, repeated illness and official matters prevented the journey, and finally the Franco-German war made it impossible to carry out the plan at all.

This memorandum is also mentioned in the same way in a letter from Wieprecht to Professor Ferdinand Sieber.

Mr Bücker now believes that he should no longer hesitate with the publication, and the publishing house is happy to comply with his offer, since the thoughts of the famous reorganizer of Prussian military bands, on the centralization of military music, will arouse the greatest interest among all armies and military music lovers and deserve the closest attention.

Chapter 1

The instrumentation of military bands

§ 1.

A well-organized military band not only forms an integral part of the entire army system of every nation, but it may also be regarded as that element of an army which, like hardly any other, lifts and strengthens the soldier's heart.

It is the soldier's most loyal companion: it leads his marches with tactful music, it inspires him with fiery sounds for the death-defying assault on the enemy, it replaces the organ for singing at the field service, it leads the departed hero to his final resting place with a plaintive funeral march and celebrates the victory he has won with jubilant tunes.

However, if a military band is to fulfil its military and musical tasks equally well, it must be well organized in terms of both the instrumentation of the voices and their training and direction—but above all in the use of suitable instruments. The following memorandum, which has emerged from the experience of forty years of loyal and enthusiastic activity in this field, will attempt to explain how this can be achieved.

§ 2.

We will first deal with the instruments that are indispensable for a military band and only suitable for it, and in the second part of this treatise we will consider the way in which the military music ensembles are organized.

In the three original instruments that have been characteristic of military bands from its earliest beginnings: the drum, the fife and the bugle, the three main factors of military music are also represented: rhythm, melody and harmony.

§ 3.

From the mass of **percussion instruments,** which even in the most ancient times had the purpose of representing the rhythmic element, our modern tenor drum has proved to be an indispensable instrument for the armies of war. Where melody and harmony are lacking, it regulates the soldier's step with a variety of rhythmic figures, calls the soldiers, tired by strenuous marches, to renewed vitality and inspires the columns to storm the enemy.

The simple drum gave rise to a whole series of other percussion instruments, of which we only mention here the hand drum[8] (tambourine), the bass drum (military timpani) and the kettle drums (timpani), all of which, with the exception of the tambourine, have found their way into military bands. It would also be appropriate to mention the triangle, the cymbals and the glockenspiel, a type of percussion instrument which—like the military timpani, which of course we had to name alongside the tenor drum[9]—came to us from the Orient, to which the name "Janissary music" still bears witness today.

§ 4.

But it was inevitable that the soldier very soon felt a desire for melody in addition to the rhythmic element. That is why he may have whistled or sung his native songs on the march at first; later this urge for melody was met more completely by the introduction of the old small transverse flute[10] in addition to the sound of the drum.

This has survived in several armies to this day because, as the simplest representative of the melodic element alongside the rhythmic

---

[8]TRANSLATOR'S NOTE: *Handtrommel,* literally a "hand drum," in this case, a tambourine.

[9]TRANSLATOR'S NOTE: *Wirbeltrommel* is usually translated as tenor drum.

[10]TRANSLATOR'S NOTE: *Querflöte,* literally the "cross-flute," meaning the transverse flute.

one, the tenor drum, it has proved to be extraordinarily effective and characteristic of field music.[11]

Of course, this simple transverse flute did not remain in use for long, but rather provided the initial impetus for the invention and introduction of a whole series of other woodwind instruments, which we divide into three classes according to their characteristic features.

The first includes:

the Flutes,

with a cylindrically drilled tube, which is divided into three different pieces—head, middle piece and foot—and in which the sound is produced directly—without a special mouthpiece.

These include: the small transverse flute, the piccolo flute in various sizes, the large flute, the flûte d'amour[12] and other minor variations of the flute.

The second class includes:

the Oboes and Bassoons,

instruments with a conically drilled tube and a mouthpiece formed by two reeds of cane striking one another.

These include the oboe, the English horn, the bassoon and the contrabassoon.

The third and final class consists of:

the Clarinets

with cylindrically bored tubing throughout and a mouthpiece cut from hard wood—beak-like—on whose beveled surface only a single reed strikes. This magnificent and extraordinarily extensive instrument, invented at the beginning of the last century by the instrument maker Christoph Denner[13] in Braunschweig, also differs from all the

---

[11]TRANSLATOR'S NOTE: *Feldmusik,* literally "field music," music played out-of-doors.

[12]TRANSLATOR'S NOTE: The *flûte d'amour,* literally "love flute", [*flauto d'amore* (Italian), *Liebesflöte* (German)] is sometimes called a mezzo-soprano flute, *flûte ténor* (French), *flauto tenore* (Italian), or *Tenorflöte* (German). It is an uncommon member of the flute family, pitched in A♭, A, or B♭ and is intermediate in size between the modern C concert flute and the alto flute in G.

[13]TRANSLATOR'S NOTE: Johann Christoph Denner (1655–1707).

reed instruments mentioned so far in that it has its fraction not on the octave but on the twelfth.

These include: the small, medium and large clarinets[14] in various sizes, the alto clarinet, the basset horn and the bass clarinet.

Since the peculiar sound effect of these three classes of wind instruments—the sharpness of the small and the delicacy of the large flutes, the pithy and cutting sound of the oboe, the sonorous timbre of the bassoon and the warm, pleasing mellifluousness of the clarinet—has proved to be quite indispensable for military bands,[15] it must also be strictly observed that this characteristic charm of the woodwind instruments is not impaired by an excess of metal additions to the keywork or even completely eliminated by trying to imitate woodwind instruments made of metal.

§ 5.

We turn to harmony, the third factor of military music, which—as we have already mentioned—finds its expression in the bugle [cornet] family.[16]

The necessity of using louder signals in the command of larger troop bodies led to the invention of the "tuba" as early as ancient times. It was a tube with a mouthpiece and bell, which was initially in a straight form, and later—because it was more manageable for military service—in a curved form,[17] and in such a form, though admittedly in many modified forms, it is still in use today in all European armies under the name cornet. Soon, alongside the old straight tuba used by the infantry, the so-called *cornua* were developed for the cavalry. These instruments had three to four bends in the tube, but later this

---

[14] TRANSLATOR'S NOTE: "Small" refers to the A♭ clarinet, "medium" the E♭ clarinet and "large" the B♭ clarinet.

[15] We have described the instruments derived from the transverse flute as preferably serving the melody, but this does not exclude the possibility that they can become equally excellent representatives of harmony in the ensemble.

[16] TRANSLATOR'S NOTE: The German "Signalhörner" translates directly as "bugle" but "cornet" is a more appropriate name for this family of instruments.

[17] The Orientals, who inherited the curved form of the tuba from the Greeks, modified it by giving the instrument the shape of the crescent, their national symbol; the Russians, who called it the flugelhorn, brought the old tuba to Germany with various modifications to the form that were more favorable for practical use.

was reduced to two bends, reaching its perfection and conclusion in the French horn.[18]

A second peculiar variety of the Greek tuba form was the *lituus*, a Roman wind instrument introduced by Tirtaeus, which contained a much longer tube, was cylindrical in the first half and conically funnel-shaped in the second half—but for riding it was constructed with an elongated circular bend—the prototype of our trumpet, which is very well perfected today.

These three classes of **brass instruments**, the bugle, the French horn and the trumpet—as they already served warlike purposes in ancient times and belonged, as it were, to the military—still form the foundation of all military bands today; for all the manifold instruments invented in more recent times, however different and strange their names may often be, are in their construction solely and exclusively variations of these three main classes.

Three types of military bands have naturally developed from them, namely:

>for the Infantry Battalions:
>cornet bands,
>for the Jäger[19] and Pionieer[20] battalions;
>a French horn band,
>for the Cavalry and Artillery Regiments:
>trumpet bands.

The many changes and modifications which the cornet, French horn and trumpet have undergone in terms of form and structure compared to the old tuba were brought about firstly by the desire to give the instrument a more manageable form, as we have already mentioned, but secondly above all by the need to enable a wider range of tones[21] and at the same time easier playability.

---

[18]This magnificent instrument, which was already used in the Middle Ages primarily for hunting signals, was first introduced to opera by Lully under the name *Cor de Chasse*.

[19]TRANSLATOR'S NOTE: Jäger ("hunter") is a German military term referring to specific light infantry units.

[20]TRANSLATOR'S NOTE: Imperial German Army Pioneers were regarded as a separate combat arm trained in construction and demolition, but they were often used as specialist infantry, serving the role of combat engineers.

[21]In the early days of its use, the tuba recta produced only two notes, namely the low octave and its next octave.

The most important invention with regard to such an expansion of the tonal range for musical purposes was the valve, which was invented in Prussia in 1816 and opened up a completely new and wide field of musical activity for brass instrumental music.

As with woodwind instruments, brass instruments are divided into three classes according to their individual construction. The first includes

the Cornet family,[22]

which have a conical tube with an oval bend and a mouthpiece that is an exact replica of the conical tube on a very small scale. These include the soprano cornet,[23] the cornet,[24] the tenor horn [UK] or alto horn [US],[25] the euphonium[26] and the tuba. The second class consists of:

the French Horn,

which, in addition to a longer, conical-funnel-shaped tube bent in a circle and ending in a plate-like bell, have a conical-funnel-shaped mouthpiece.

These include: the Natural French horn, the Invention French horn,[27] the Valve French horn, the Soprano (French) horn, the Alto

---

[22] TRANSLATOR'S NOTE: We quote here a paragraph from Curt Sachs, *The History of Musical Instruments*, (New York: W. W. Norton, 1940), pp. 431–432, to clarify the confusion surrounding the "cornet" family:

> All these cornets, flügelhorns, alto horns, baritones, euphoniums, bass and contrabass tubas were constructed in different countries by different "inventors" between 1825 and 1845 as they were needed in orchestra and band, but with no intention of forming a homogenous family. Following the general tendency of the nineteenth century, the Franco–Belgian instrument maker Adolphe Sax in Paris united them in 1843 under the name *saxhorns* and gave them a uniform model.

[23] TRANSLATOR'S NOTE: The modern *soprano cornet* in E♭, called the *cornetino* by Wieprecht, was also known as the *sopranino cornet* in E♭, the *piston* or *piccolo*.

[24] TRANSLATOR'S NOTE: The modern cornet pitched in B♭.

[25] TRANSLATOR'S NOTE: Also called the *Alt-Cornet* (*Altkornett*) in German, *bugle alto* in French, *flicorno alto* in Italian, pitched in B♭, can be coiled in shape like a trumpet or upright like a tuba.

[26] TRANSLATOR'S NOTE: *Baryton* (*bariton-Tuba*) in German.

[27] TRANSLATOR'S NOTE: In 1754, Anton Josef Hampel (1710–1771) designed a horn with the manufacturer Johann Georg Werner in Dresden, called the *Invention-*

(French) horn, the Tenor (French) horn, the Baritone (French) horn, the Bass (French) horn and the Contrabass (French) horn.

The third class is occupied by:

the Trumpets,

whose medium-sized tube, also elongated but only bent once, has a cylindrical conical-funnel-shaped construction and a turned cup-shaped mouthpiece. These include: the Signal Trumpet, the Invention Trumpet, the Keyed Trumpet, the Slide Trumpet, the Valve Trumpet; the Slide Trombone in Alto, Tenor and Bass, which, like the Slide Trumpet, makes a complete scale possible by slightly shifting the tube and can therefore do without any valves; finally the Tenor (Valve) Trumpet, also known as the Tenor Horn.[28]

§ 6.

Even if the various musical genres must be allowed to borrow individual instruments from each other in order to expand their ensembles, the mouthpieces must under no circumstances be interchanged, since the timbre and original character of an instrument is determined precisely by the fact that it retains its own mouthpiece.

At this point we would like to mention a number of other shortcomings which, to the best of our conviction, are not at all conducive to military bands. These include, above all, the unjustified use of valves for the magnificent slide trombone. After all, the slides enable the greatest evenness of sound in all pitches and at the same time such pure intonation as is characteristic of bowed instruments. At the expense of the basic character of the trombone, the valves allow a volubility which is not at all in keeping with the solemn nature of this instrument.

Equally inadmissible is the introduction of certain colossi of bass-wind instruments which bear no relation at all to the human form

---

Waldhorn. This horn had pitched crooks designed to fit in the center of the body, held in place by a pin.

[28] The author of this memorandum considers the name tenor trumpet to be more appropriate—although he himself habitually used the term tenor horn in his scores—in order to avoid any confusion with the circularly curved tenor horn listed under the horns.

and virtually mock the player's lung power by requiring a new breath for almost every single note.

Also, the bell should only be raised on those instruments whose range makes a more manageable shape necessary, such as bassoons and tubas; on the other instruments, however, with the exception of French horns, it should always be directed straight ahead.

§ 7.

If we now summarize once again all the instruments of all classes that appear indispensable for military bands, these are all instruments that also belong to chamber, orchestral and opera music, while we generally exclude all those instruments from the military band that are not adopted by other orchestral music. For we believe that it is truly one of the most beautiful blessings of the cultivation of military bands that it forms, as it were, a popular instrumental teaching institute from which all other and higher branches of instrumental music can be recruited.

These instruments listed here can be found in all civilized armies, albeit with different names and slight modifications. Thus the instrument called cornetino in northern Germany is called ottavin in southern Germany, the soprano cornet—high flugelhorn, alto cornet—alto flugelhorn, tenor horn—bass flugelhorn, baritone tuba—euphonium, bass tuba—bombardon or helicon, contrabassoon—harmonie bass or tritonicon, the French horn is called horn for short; the clarinets, distinguished there according to size as small, medium and large, are named here according to tuning, and probably other things as well. The point remains the same.

From all these instruments it is now quite possible to put together a standard instrumentation for every kind of military band, which satisfies all, even the highest demands of tonal performance.

In the following tables I have made what I believe, after much thought and many attempts, to be a successful attempt to create such a standard instrumentation.

Note: In these tables: Pr. = Primo, Sec. = Secondo, T. = Terzo, Qu. = Quarto.

A. Cornet Band
for
Infantry Battalions and Regiments.

Instrument	per Battalion	per Regiment	Tuning	Alternative tuning
Soprano cornet	1	3	E♭	D
Cornet	2 Pr. / 1 Sec.	5 Pr. / 4 Sec.	B♭	A
Tenor horn (UK) / Alto horn (US)	1 Pr. / 1 Sec.	3 Pr. / 3 Sec.	E♭	D
Baritone	1 Pr. / 1 Sec.	3 Pr. / 3 Sec.	B♭	A
Euphonium	1	3		
Bass tuba	1 Pr. / 2 Sec.	3 Pr. / 2 Sec.		
Total	12	36		

Note: The cornets (flugelhorns), tenor horns (bass flugelhorns), baritone and bass tubas (euphoniums, bombardons and helicons) can also be represented by the so-called saxhorns which are common in military music in France, England and Spain.

B. French Horn Band
for
Jäger and Pioneer Battalions.

Instrument	Musicians	Signal trumpeters to reinforce the Music Corps	Total	Tuning	Alternative tuning
Soprano cornet	1	1	2	E♭	D
Cornet	1 Pr. 1 Sec.	2	4	B♭	A
Tenor horn (UK) Alto horn (US)	1 Pr. 1 Sec.	2	4	E♭	D
Baritone	1 Pr. 1 Sec.	2	4	B♭	A
Euphonium	1 Pr. 1 Sec.		2	B♭	A
Bass tuba	1 Pr. 1 Sec.	2	4		
French horn	1 Pr. 1 Sec. 1 T.	3	6	F	E
Trumpet	1 Pr. 1 Sec. 1 T.		3	F	E
Total	17	12	29		

Note: For French horn bands, with the exception of the soprano cornet and the trumpet, the circular form of the French horn is intended for all instruments.

C. Trumpet Band
for
Cavalry and Artillery Regiments.

Instrument	Cavalry	Artillery			Tuning	Alternative tuning
		riding	on foot	per Regiment on foot		
Soprano cornet	2	1	1	3	E♭	D
Cornet	2 Pr. 2 Sec.	2	2	6	B♭	A
Tenor horn (UK) Alto horn (US)	1 Pr. 1 Sec.	2	1	3	E♭	D
Baritone	1 Pr. 1 Sec.	2	2	6	B♭	A
Euphonium	2	1	1	3		
Bass tuba	2 Pr. 2 Sec.	2	2	6		
Trumpet	3 Pr. 2 Sec. 2 T. 2 Qu.	4	4	12	E♭	D
Total	25	14	13	39		

Note: On cavalry and artillery trumpets, it must be possible to quickly and easily remove the valve mechanism and use a simple bugle for signaling purposes.

D. Janissary Music[29]
for
Infantry Regiments.

In addition to the soprano cornet, this also contains all the brass instruments mentioned above and is therefore composed as follows:

Soprano cornet 1 pr. 1 sec., tenor horn (UK) 1 pr. 1 sec., baritone 1 pr. 1 sec., euphonium 1, bass tuba 2 pr. 2 sec., French horn 1 pr. 1 sec., trumpet 1 pr. 1 sec. 1 t. 1 qu., flute, small and large, each 1 pr. 1 sec., oboe 1 pr. 1 sec, small clarinet (A♭) 1, medium clarinet (E♭) 1 pr. 1 sec., large clarinet (B♭) 4 pr. 4 sec., bassoon 3, contrabassoon 2, tenor trombone 2, bass trombone 2, triangle or bells 1, field drum 2, cymbals 1 pair, bass drum 1. In total, therefore: 46.[30]

The richness of this instrumental ensemble enables the faithful reproduction—even with retention of the key—of any orchestral work and puts an end to the monotony that unfortunately still prevails in many places where compositions do not progress any further in modulation than the E♭ tuning with its nearest related keys.

Incidentally, the E♭ tuning corresponds most closely to the military service.

---

[29]TRANSLATOR'S NOTE: This *Janissary Music* equates to our modern wind band or concert band.

[30]TRANSLATOR'S NOTE: I interpret this as 48 players, however, the original text says 46.

Chapter 2

Organization of the music ensembles

§ 1.

Number of bandsmen and musicians[31]

The entire group of musicians are divided into three classes: drummers and signallers, trumpeters, and hautboisten.[32] We will now first have to assign to each troop type the class of bandsmen belonging to it.

Let us first look at the

Infantry

A regiment (of 3 battalions, 12 companies = 3000 men) will need the following signalmen: 1 conductor [*Stabshornisten*],[33] and per battalion 1 drum major, 8 drummers, 12 signallers; thus per regiment 63 men.

---

[31] TRANSLATOR'S NOTE: A distinction is made between the musicians and the bandsmen (*Spielleute*). The bandsmen have to give the signals and belong to the rank and file of the companies, while the musicians belong to the regimental staff. Only the trumpeters of the cavalry are also required to perform signals.

[32] TRANSLATOR'S NOTE: The term *hautboist* (pronounced "oboist") was first used to refer to a woodwind player (after *hautbois*, the French term for the oboe). From the Classical era onwards, hautboist was also an officer rank in the orchestra and in classical wind music. The title gradually became detached from the instruments actually played: in Prussia Frederick William I dissolved the court trumpet corps in 1713 and assigned the trumpeters to his Hautboist ensembles, turning them into infantry musicians. Later, the term *hoboist* was used to refer to a military musician in a music corps. In the infantry of the German army, the word was in use until around the First World War.

[33] *Stabshornisten*, literally *Staff Bugler*.

If we add to this the regimental band with 1 bandmaster and 46 hautboisten,[34] this gives a total of 100 men per regiment.

Likewise, a Jäger or Pionieer battalion (800 men strong) includes: 1 conductor [*Stabshornisten*], 17 musicians and 12 signallers, making a total of 30 men.

If we now turn to the cavalry and artillery, each

Cavalry Regiment

is composed of five squadrons, with five trumpeters required per squadron; 1 conductor [*Stabstrompeter*] and 25 trumpeters per regiment.

Finally with the

Artillery

per regiment a) for the mounted detachment 1 conductor and 16 trumpeters; b) for the artillery on foot, in three detachments: 1 conductor [*Stabstrompeter*] and 39 trumpeters, i.e. 13 men per detachment, making a total of 57 men.

§ 2.

Requirements with regard to the performance capabilities of the entire bandsmen and musicians.

1. The drum major

must himself be an excellent drummer, as he has to teach the drums practically, without sheet music, only by ear, in the execution of the prescribed drum strokes.

2. The conductor [*Stabshornist*] of the regiment

has to take care of the musical training of the signallers by teaching them how to handle the instrument and how to form the natural tones on the brass family, and then all the elementary knowledge that seems necessary for the execution of both the signals and larger

---

[34] TRANSLATOR'S NOTE: The hautboisten were generally wind players who were also capable of doubling on a string instrument.

musical performances, in which some of the musicians have to play the tenor and bass parts.

If the ability to read music quickly is highly desirable for marches and other musical performances, it is even more important from a strategic point of view, as the signals can be changed at will at the order of the commander and can be used immediately in the field.[35]

By acquiring this skill, the signallers are prepared for any higher musical performance for which the conductor has to instruct them.

The conductor must also instruct the signallers in the use of all the chromatic brass instruments assigned to the various parts of the band. It is only through the use of the valve brass instruments that the ability to perform marches, chorales and songs, and even higher musical tasks, is established.

If the conductor is a well-trained musician and a skillful elementary teacher, the signallers can easily be taught to perform good marches from reading sheet music within a year.

At the end of his military service, however, every signaller who wants to capitulate and stay with music will certainly have matured to become a principal hautboisten or trumpeter.

This shows how important the cultivation of signallers must be, since it is actually a preliminary school and the safest means of recruitment for the entire military music system of an army.

The organization of signallers in the Royal Prussian Army was initiated by the author of this memorandum as early as 1837.

We have him to thank for the fact that in 1861, within 6 months, 32 brass bands of 22 men each and 10 trumpet bands of 16 men each could be established for the newly formed regiments.

Is it not characteristic that, while in other large state armies the music corps is currently being forced to disband completely due to a lack of music ensembles in the cavalry, artillery and even in the Jäger battalions, while in the Royal Prussian Army military music is in full bloom in all parts of the troops?

---

[35] This ability to sight-read fluently is characteristic of the cavalry trumpeters of the Royal Prussian Army without exception.

3. The regimental bandmaster

must not only have an excellent musical education and knowledge of the entire instrumental world, but must also be experienced in many military matters.

He is required to know the drum strokes, signals, marches of the drums in ensemble with the fifes, the taps, the cadences of the presentation and defile marches, etc., as prescribed in the drill regulations, so that he is able to ensure that no erroneous notes creep in. He is the supreme musical authority in the regiment, to whom the conductors, the drum major, as well as all the signalmen and hautboisten have to submit. The regimental bandmaster must therefore also focus his attention on the musical training of the signallers, organize and supervise music lessons according to a specific syllabus, give his conscientious opinion on the purchase of instruments and music materials and, finally, guide the regimental band in its performance to the highest possible level of musical efficiency.

However, a man who is expected to perform such a wide range of activities and who is burdened with such a great responsibility must in any case be assigned a higher rank than that of a non-commissioned officer.

4. The hautboisten

must, without exception, be practically trained musicians and, in particular, know how to play the instrument assigned to them in the corps.

In addition, they must also be able to play some kind of stringed instrument, as the regimental bandmaster is nowadays responsible for chamber, salon and dance orchestra music in all places.

Apart from the often very fruitful acquisition of musicians, such care of the string orchestra gives the regimental band a higher reputation in the eyes of art connoisseurs and, above all, exerts a powerful influence on the formation of good taste and musical sense among the inhabitants of the garrisons concerned.

THE MILITARY BAND   55

5. The conductor [*Stabshornist*] for the Jäger and Pioneer French horn band

has—like the conductor of the infantry—a theoretical training in the art of music. He is also responsible for the musical training of the signallers, whereby he may make use of the very important help of his band musicians.

6. The musicians of the French horn band

must know how to play the brass instrument assigned to them in the corps to perfection and be trained in prima vista[36] playing, in addition—as we already presuppose with the infantry's hautboisten—also have training in the treatment of any stringed instrument, so that the conductor is able to organize a reasonable string ensemble from his 17 trained musicians.

The Jäger and Pioneer bands, which in addition to the signallers also enjoys the support of 17 specialist musicians, must of course be able to meet much higher artistic demands.

7. The conductor [*Stabstrompeter*] of the trumpet Band

Probably no military musician is expected to meet greater demands in terms of the dual skills of the soldier and the musician than the regimental conductor. He should be completely at home in all branches of cavalry service and perform excellently in the reproduction of signals on foot and on horseback.

It may well be assumed that he must have an excellent training in the art of music, both as a performer of his instrument and as an arranger for his trumpet corps when he takes up his position, but the other side of his professional activity, that of the strict and capable soldier, can only be acquired after several years of practical service. For this reason, the rank of conductor must always be trained and supplemented from the ranks of the trumpeters.

His activity in the field is of the greatest importance. He must not leave his commanding officer for a moment in front of the regiment, must, riding at his side, take all his commands correctly, sound the

---

[36]TRANSLATOR'S NOTE: Prima vista—sight reading, performing a piece of music straight from the music notation without rehearsal.

signal in question with lightning speed and then have it spread over the whole regiment by the trumpeters who have been assigned to the squadrons.

Boldly facing death, he must not allow himself to be distracted by anything, since the slightest mistake, the smallest misunderstanding would have the most unpredictable consequences to the detriment of the whole.

As strict as the conductor appears as a soldier in front of the regiment, he must be just as lenient towards his trumpeters as a music master.

The performing art of music can only flourish under a mild regiment; not military force but only thorough instruction can one awaken the love and enthusiasm for (ensemble) music without which the performing musicians would only ever bear the stamp of musical dressage.

The conductor of the artillery on foot has 39 musicians at his disposal for the organization of his music, which he has to divide up and fill in their parts in such a way that each section of the regiment with its 13 men simultaneously gains a complete trumpet band. It is obvious that these three sections must have exactly the same number of voices so that they are able to form a large ensemble when the regiment is united—without any preparation.

The conductor must also make his arrangements accordingly and ensure that the same principles are followed even when the sections are separated into different garrisons. He will also be responsible for suggesting suitable trumpeters to the regimental command for the leadership of the 2nd and 3rd sections.

8. The trumpeter

A young man in the cavalry and artillery must, on joining the regiment, demonstrate musical ability on any of the instruments associated with a trumpet band, as well as in sight reading.

Learning the trumpet signals can therefore be left to him. He will need no further instruction for this except for a few waves from the conductor and the presentation of the notation of the drill regulations.

It is also highly desirable for the trumpeter to play a string or woodwind instrument of some kind so that, in addition to brass music, an orchestra with stringed instruments can be created for the performance of salon and dance music, which will provide enjoyment for the officer corps and the inhabitants of the garrison town in question, and often quite significant private income for the trumpeters.

The cavalry and artillery regiments cannot, apart from the necessary signalmen, have special music corps on horseback, so the signal trumpeters must also combine the soldier and musician in one person. Since soldierly training—training on foot, guard duty, instruction lessons, then learning to ride, fence and shoot—requires a considerable amount of time and can only be gained in practical service with the regiment, there is absolutely no time left for thorough musical instruction for the signal trumpeters—as was possible in the infantry—especially since cavalry music is in possession of much richer instrumental resources than just signalling and is therefore on a much higher artistic level.

It is therefore essential to recruit practically trained musicians for the organization of this type of music, and where such are lacking, not to shy away from even small sacrifices in functional allowances.

§ 3.

The centralization of army music

The author has been striving for this for many years and has achieved it by finally producing the above instrumentations attached to this memorandum—provided, of course, that there is as little deviation from the prescribed instrumentation for all parts of the army as from the other provisions of the Ministry of War.

The task of carrying out, directing and supervising such centralization of army music in all directions would, however, have to be assigned to a musical head of the most comprehensive expertise, an army bandmaster in charge of the Ministry of War, because just as the signal system is centralized by presenting the notation in the drill regulations, this can also be done with all army music if all marches, chorales, hymns, etc. are written according to the instrumentations suggested, are orchestrated in accordance with the instrumentations and made available to all troop commands in one and the same score from the central office by means of mechanical reproduction.

This not only makes it possible for each individual music corps to play a piece of music according to the instructions in an exemplary manner, but also for several, even many music corps of the most diverse musical genres, united into smaller, larger, even gigantically reinforced ensembles, to perform the same piece of music together without any preparation.[37]

Since the War Ministry is responsible not only for all regulations concerning the budget and pension entitlements for the various ranks of bandsmen and musicians in the army, but also for the regulations concerning the publication of signals, army marches and all other pieces of music for the army, it will become an indispensable condition that the entire field of army music be assigned to a department in the Ministry of War, which, under the supervision of the army bandmaster, must oversee all matters pertaining to it, and in particular the appointment of military music corps leaders—probably the most important element of military music.

Just as the commoner who wishes to remain in the army beyond his term of service is offered the prospect of advancement to private, sergeant, sergeant-major or sergeant-at-arms, or even, if he has the knowledge, a higher rank, e.g. that of paymaster, a corresponding advancement would have to be made in the same way for the musicians, namely from drummer or signaller as a commoner, to musical trumpeter as a private, from this to hautboisten or trumpeter as a non-commissioned officer, from this to conductor [*Stabshornisten, Stabshautboisten* or *Stabstrompeter*] as a sergeant or sergeant-at-arms, and finally from the latter grade to regimental bandmaster with the rank of regimental paymaster.

If it is therefore assumed that the music conductor aspirants may only emerge from the principal hautboisten or trumpeters, it will be regarded as a special reward for faithful military service if the War Ministry transfers the best-behaved, most capable musicians, proven in every military virtue, to a conservatory for the purpose of higher training in the art of music, from where they then—with simultaneous service advancement—return to the army.

---

[37]Tasks of this kind in music offer no difficulties in the Royal Prussian Army. Thanks to such centralization, ensemble music performances of more than 1000 musicians have often taken place in the army.

These would be the basic features according to which a school-appropriate army music must be organized. If they were to take root generally, if military music (which is recognized as a separate, independent instrumental branch of the art of music in all educated armies) were to be given the same unshakeable basis, especially through the general introduction of my instrumentation, as is already the case with chamber orchestral music—whose instrumental means are generally recognized and sanctioned for the whole musical world—then this would truly be the highest reward for my forty years of faithful and enthusiastic work in this field of the art of music.

Berlin, November 6, 1868.
W. Wieprecht,
Director of all the music of the Guard Corps, etc.

Appendix

Wieprecht's report on the victory of the band of the Prussian Guards at the international competition of European military music at the Paris World Exhibition.

On Sunday, 21 July 1867, the international competition was held at the Palace of Industry.[38] As early as 10 o'clock in the morning, the crowd of onlookers began to surge in front of the barracks where we were located; the Parisians wanted to see the foreign music corps in their parade uniforms marching off to their destination.

The competition hall formed an elongated quadrangle, in the center of which were decorated benches for all the music corps. These seats were surrounded by a fragrant flowerbed of the most beautiful plants, behind which was a wide, terraced passage. From this passage, the boxes of the audience extended like terraces to both ends of the hall, which was decorated with emblems and coats of arms. At one end of the hall were the imperial court boxes, which were adjoined on both sides by the boxes of the highest state officials and legations. In front of these boxes was a large table for the jury, equipped with the necessary writing materials. A short distance away, directly in front of the jury, the orchestra stand was set up at an appropriate height. At the other end of the hall there was a large box-like platform as a meeting place for the entire music corps. The latter arranged

---

[38]TRANSLATOR'S NOTE: The Palace of Industry (*Palais de l'Industrie*) was an exhibition hall located in Paris between the Seine River and the Champs-Élysées, which was erected for the Paris World Fair in 1855.

themselves here to march off to the benches intended for them, after a previous call.

1. The Baden Music Corps, under the direction of its bandmaster Burg (54 musicians).

2. First Regiment of the Spanish Engineers, under the command of its bandmaster Maimo (64 musicians).

3. Music Corps of the Prussian Guards, under the leadership of Meinberg and Saro and their chief Wieprecht (85 musicians). The woodwinds consisted of 4 flutes, 4 oboes, 6 bassoons, 4 contrabassoons, 1 small bassoon, 4 middle bassoons and 16 large clarinets. In terms of brass instruments, we had 4 soprano cornets, 4 alto cornets, 4 French horns, 4 tenor horns, 2 baritone tubas, 6 bass tubas, 8 trumpets and 8 slide trombones. As for percussion instruments, we had 2 snare drums, 1 bass drum, 2 pairs of cymbals, 1 glockenspiel and a triangle, a total of 85 instruments.

4. The Austrian 73rd Regiment Duke of Württemberg under the direction of bandmaster Zimmermann (76 musicians).

5. The Belgian Grenadier Regiment, under the bandmaster M. C. Bender (59 musicians).

6. The Bavarian First Infantry Regiment under its bandmaster Siebenkaes (51 musicians).

7. Dutch Grenadier and Chasseur Regiments, under K.-M. Dunkler (56 musicians).

8. The Russian Chevalier Guard under the leadership of the Corps Bandmaster Doerfeld (71 men).

9. Guide de la garde Imperiale, conductor Cressonois (62 musicians).

10. Garde de Paris, conductor Paulus (56 musicians).

The corps marched down from the balcony into the parterre of the hall in the order in which they were to take their seats in the designated places. The Baden musicians first mounted the bandstand and began with the Adagio of the *Overture to Oberon*. The musicians, however, although they had all taken up their instruments, were not heard by the audience. The 40,000 listeners looked with rapt attention at the musicians, whose technical gesticulations they noticed but whose playing they could not hear. There was a general grumbling, a tumultuous noise, banging and shouting: "We don't hear any music! Put the band in the middle of the hall!" The latter wish was, however, impossible for the time being. The musicians finished the Adagio of the overture and instead played the finale from Mendelssohn's *Loreley*, which relied more on the effect of the ensemble than the Adagio of the *Oberon* overture did, with the noise and pounding from the audience continuing until the end. This was followed by the performance of the *Oberon* overture, which, however, passed without a trace amidst the uninterrupted noise of the audience. However, the attentive listener could not fail to notice that this music corps possessed very capable musically trained forces, which would certainly have found their well-deserved recognition under more favorable circumstances.

Under such unfortunate circumstances, the Spaniards entered the bandstand and began a *Fantasia on Spanish National Songs*,[39] which was followed by the competition set piece.[40] This music, too, disappeared without a trace amid continued unrest and loud dissatisfaction from the audience.

It had not escaped my notice that the music corps had completely misunderstood the purpose of their task and, in the opinion that they were to perform a large military concert here, had completely confused the aim of playing in front of a jury. Instead of facing the jury, they faced the audience. The length of the hall caused not only an echo, but a complete echo of at least the scale by a whole quarter note of the bar. We therefore faced the jury during our performance, and I alone as conductor faced the audience; the sound of our instruments thus gained a very short distance. After all, the purpose of this whole competition was to test military music and not to give a military concert in front of an audience of 40,000 people, which would have included at least enlisting more musicians to fulfill the latter purpose.

---

[39] TRANSLATOR'S NOTE: *Fantasie sur des airs nationaux* by Gevaert.

[40] TRANSLATOR'S NOTE: Weber's *Overture to Oberon* was the set piece, however, bands played different transcriptions.

We began with my *Fantasy on The Prophet*[41] which is precisely calculated for the sound effect of a military band. Just by changing our position, we attracted the attention of the audience and a gradual calm set in among them. The moment was even more favorable for us in the strong unison of all instruments, with which my fantasy begins, which already in the 7th bar flows into a harmony sounding *fortissimo*. Here the audience was gripped by a coherent musical effect from all sides and the words: "Silence, silence, what beautiful music!" resounded from all sides! A great calm ensued, under which every, even the finest nuance of the players could be heard. Before the final movement of the fantasia, my solo cornetist was rewarded for the execution of his prescribed cadenza by a never-ending round of applause, and I almost feared that the desired calm would not return and that our music would be robbed of its most beautiful laurel. However, the audience realized from my bows that the piece of music had not yet ended; they became quieter, so that we were able to successfully finish the fantasy with extraordinary silence in the hall.

Now it was time for the main task of the concert, namely the performance of the *Oberon* overture. The musical intelligence of our principal players had understood that nothing could be achieved in that immense space by the prescribed *piano* passages of the Adagio; at my suggestion, the *pianos,* which I had prepared to execute with muted instruments, were played open. The Allegro of the overture was performed very fierily and at a very lively tempo. A never-ending applause from all sides, which even the gentlemen of the jury expressed by rising from their seats, accompanied our performance at its conclusion.

Happy and cheerful, we left the grandstand and returned to our old seats. Now the Austrians took the stage, and their colossal bass instruments, the tremendous bombardons, helicons, etc., gave us a mighty fright, all the more so because a prevailing affection favored the Austrians. They sensed the flawed positioning of the Spanish, etc., took the same position as we had taken in a modified way; they began with Rossini's *William Tell Overture.* Even if it cannot be denied that intonation and ensemble met the artistic requirements, this was not the case with regard to the musical concept. The beautiful solo of the English horn in the Andante pastorale was played on a flugelhorn.

---

[41]TRANSLATOR'S NOTE: *Fantasie sur le Prophète*, of Meyerbeer.

The Austrian band has neither oboe nor bassoon and this musical mistake was pointed out. The combination of the two English horn solos with the flute was, since the former had to be played on a flugelhorn, an unsuitable one, at least in Paris, where the composer lives and his presence at the concert could be assumed. Likewise, the sound of the instruments did not match their unnatural size. The overall sound effect was somewhat muted and extremely short.

In the performance of dances and defile marches, potpourris, etc., the Austrians have achieved a mastery that is probably unmatched by any of the other music corps present. Anything beyond that, namely classical music, is based on the shortest staccato in all situations, like dance music. Otherwise, their military music is characteristic and appropriate for its purpose. The Austrians were also greeted with much applause from the audience.

Now the Belgians came forward—wonderfully equipped, like the Bavarians and Dutch, with large string contrabasses and kettledrums. They began with a fantasia on themes from the opera *William Tell,* the final movement of which was the allegro of the *William Tell Overture.* The audience thus had the pleasure of enjoying the *Tell* and *Oberon* overtures twice in succession. The Belgian military band, which I had got to know 25 years ago and whose competition seemed to me the most dangerous, passed by in a strangely meaningless way, although it seemed to me that their wind players were well-trained musicians; it lacked the military character, which it completely lost sight of, which is explained by the use of string instruments and kettledrums.

The Bavarians followed this with a *Fantasy* on home airs,[42] which greatly exceeded the time limit, so that they immediately lost the necessary calm in the audience again. The *Oberon* overture was not performed with the delicacy and poetic effusion required by the work.

The Dutch now followed with the performance of a *Fantasia* on themes from Gounod's *Faust.*[43] The audience's attention for the subject matter had already diminished to such an extent that their per-

---

[42]TRANSLATOR'S NOTE: Wieprecht calls this work the *Phantasie über Heimathslüfte,* however, Oscar Comettant, in his book *La musique de la garde républicaine en Amérique,* says this work was the *Introduction et choeur nuptial de Lohengrin* by Wagner. It's possible Wieprecht mixed up this one with the *Fantasie sur des airs nationaux* by Gevaert performed by the Spanish.

[43]TRANSLATOR'S NOTE: *Fantaisie sur Faust,* Gounod.

formance did not receive the recognition it deserved; in general, the pieces were all too long in terms of time.

Now the Russians came to the fore. Their appearance, in terms of clothing and decoration with their armored helmets, made an imposing impression and revived the interest of the audience to some extent. They played a fantasy of their own choice: *Overture from A Life for the Tsar* by Glinka. This overture was more in the form of a fantasy of Russian national songs. They were beautifully performed in a truly nationalistic manner. The overall effect of this music was characteristically military, although the performance of its musical parts could have expressed more warmth. This can be said in particular of the *Oberon* overture, which was also performed at an extremely slow tempo. The efficiency of this music corps was indeed all the more surprising as the general opinion prevailed that the Russians had not yet progressed as far as other nations in the art of instrumental music.

The moment finally arrived when the inventions of the instrument maker Sax were to receive their sanction before the whole world as a result of this competition. The two corps representing these inventions were the *Guide de la garde Imperiale* and the *Garde de Paris*. The first corps played a wittily composed fantasy on the *Carnival of Venice* by Charles Collin. This fantasy contained highly interesting instrumental effects, which were executed with extraordinary virtuosity. The whole thing was performed in a highly humorous style, so that this piece of music could very well be described as a—fantasy burlesque. The character of military music, however, was very far removed from this music, so that one might claim that military music had already completely merged into virtuosity. This kind of music belongs more in a salon than in front of a regiment.

The second music corps also performed as their own choice the *Bridal Chorus and March* from the opera *Lohengrin*. The chorus and march made a beautiful impression. The introduction, which the composer wrote with nothing but mutes in the orchestra, and which was whispered by the saxophones), was also not suitable for illustrating a military band. Even if the extraordinary virtuosity and precision with which these pieces were performed cannot be denied, music that is supposed to inspire the warrior's courage for battle and victory does not require such means.

It was probably quite natural that after a five-hour performance in which one was forced to listen to the *Oberon Overture* ten times, the audience would become exhausted. This is precisely the reason, or the misguided direction, to which French military music has paid homage for 25 years, that the performance of their own compatriots was no longer able to enthuse in the same way as the Prussians and Austrians had succeeded in doing. In general, it has become a maxim in the last three decades to allow industrialists to exploit the tools of military music for the benefit of the latter. Orchestral chamber music, in its harmony of flutes, oboes, bassoons, clarinets, French horns and trombones, possesses these instruments, which are so excellently suited to military music and which, with the addition of modern chromatic brass instruments, e.g. the cornets in soprano and alto, the tenor horns, the baritone and bass tubas, finally with the addition of the usual percussion instruments, form such an infinitely rich and beautiful instrumentation for a military band that it does not require all new inventions, which are after all are only variations of these, to produce a characteristic and powerful sounding military band.[44]

The last music corps left the bandstand at 6:30 PM. Everyone, audience and musicians alike, waited in eager anticipation for the decision. At this moment the Royal Danish Consul, Mr Bamberg, member of the jury, approached the Prussian Music Corps with great excitement, announcing that we had won the first grand prize according to the jury's decision. At the same time, the secretary of the competition committee, Mr Jonas, approached me with the request to go with him to General Mellenet. We had to make our way across the bandstand to get to the jury. When we both arrived there, all the members of the jury had disappeared; they had retired to an adjoining room for a second consultation. Mr Jonas was astonished at this disappearance of the jury and asked me to wait a moment and not to leave the place so that he could find me again. I followed his request, but unfortunately in vain. After a good half hour, during which the audience had already grown impatient with the long wait for the result to be announced, the members of the committee appeared on a balcony in the middle of the hall and General Mellenet announced the following: The jury felt compelled to deviate from the old program for certain reasons, in that one grand prize, to which 2000 francs were added, was replaced by three grand prizes of 2500 francs each, a second prize

---

[44]TRANSLATOR'S NOTE: I take this to be Wieprecht's indictment of the French use of saxophones in the military band.

of 2000 francs was added, and finally a third prize of 1000 francs was determined. He designated the first 3 grand prizes in alphabetical order so as not to give preference to any of the winners. 1. for the Austrians; 2. for the French; 3. for the Prussians; for the Russians the prize of the supplement 2000 francs; for the Dutch the prize of 1000 francs. Thus ended this memorable contest, from which only the Prussians emerged victorious.

On the 30th (Tuesday) a marching performance took place before His Majesty the Emperor and his entire entourage in the Tuilleries Garden at 5 o'clock in the evening. At the end of the performance, the entire music corps had to form a closed circle. His Majesty and his entourage personally distributed medals to the foreign officers in command, as well as to all the regimental bandmasters present. Here I had the honor of receiving the Knight's Cross of the Legion of Honor from the hand of the Emperor in the most flattering recognition of my merits in the field of military music. The corps and all those present gave the Emperor three thunderous cheers. The carré fell back into line and the music corps began their march. That evening I was delighted to receive an invitation to the imperial table, where the Emperor talked to me at length about the nature of military music, asked me many questions and expressed his regret that he did not have in writing everything I had told him about this subject. On leaving, I promised to write a memorandum on the organization of military music in an army. (This memorandum is now known to our readers.)

www.ingramcontent.com/pod-product-compliance
Lightning Source LLC
Chambersburg PA
CBHW060540080526
44586CB00012B/801